Praise For
Planning a Prayer Retreat

Practical, specific, doable, valuable. These are words that came to my mind as I read *Planning a Prayer Retreat* by my friend, Deborah Miller. I've known Deborah for over 20 years and have always appreciated her walk with the Lord and her perspective on how to please Him.

Most books on prayer are designed to increase our personal prayer life. This book is different. It shows the value and the power of joining our prayers with the prayers of others. But it goes beyond that. It also addresses very practical aspects of how to make it happen. Who should be invited? Where should we go? How long should we be there? What about meals? How do we start? How do we know what to pray for? Dr. Miller addresses these and many other practical issues so you can get a running start at how to help others experience the joy of meaningful prayer times with others. This book is not only worth reading, it is worth doing.

—**Dennis Fuqua**, Director, *International Renewal Ministries.*

***

Planning a Prayer Retreat: An Easy Step-by-Step Guide for Organizing and Leading Group Prayer Retreats is a fabulous resource for anyone seeking to lead others in an organized prayer experience. Having commissioned Deborah to lead a prayer retreat for my leadership team, I have experienced the personal fruit from the Spirit's revelation to Deborah. This book is a tool birthed from her personal experience, wisdom, and the Holy Spirit's leading. It masterfully combines practical strategies with profound insights, empowering facilitators to create an experience that when followed, works time and time again. Deborah's thoughtful approach not only offers step-by-step guidance but also inspires readers to embrace the sacredness of prayer in community. Whether you're a seasoned leader or new to the concept of *planning a prayer retreat*, this guide is a valuable tool that will enrich your experience and the experience of your participants. Highly recommended!
—**Abby Conger,** Women's Pastor, *Vancouver Church, Vancouver, WA*

***

What do popcorn, a prayer topic, and the Holy Spirit have in common? According to Dr. Deborah Miller they create a prayer strategy to facilitate group intercessory prayer that assists people hearing from the Lord while listening to one another for intentional prayer that is "dynamic and engaging." If you have ever led a group of people in prayer, I believe this practical

and insightful book will be instructive whether you find yourself wanting to lead a group prayer retreat or not. Includes explanations for the purpose and critical use of time during prayer sessions, resistance to prayer, debriefing prayer sessions as well as potential scenarios of 'what ifs' of spiritual leadership while facilitating prayer. This book is pure encouragement and inspiration to pray supplied from a clear biblical foundation in Chapter 2 with more references and support found throughout the book. Miller calls the reader to relationship with God and others through prayer and to connect with God through prayer corporately.
—**Judy L. Glanz**, PhD, Spiritual Director, *Facilitator Guided Silence and Solitude Retreats*

***

Lots of us know why we should pray together, and lots of us want to do it. But we struggle with knowing how to do it – and Dr. Miller offers a helpful guide to help us get there. Her step-by-step resource offers passion, wisdom, and practical steps for any leader longing to pull people into deeper experiences of prayer together.
—**Rev. Michaele LaVigne**, Director of the *Spiritual Formation Initiative at Nazarene Theological Seminary*

***

Planning a Prayer Retreat is like a Swiss army knife - there is something for most everyone. If you would like to hold a prayer retreat but have no idea where to start or what to do, you will find answers here. If, like me, you have led MANY prayer retreats, what Deborah Miller has put together will help you think in a fresh, creative way about what you are doing, and why. I wish this resource was available decades ago!

—**Mike Higgs**, member, *National Prayer Committee;*
24-7 Prayer USA; North American Prayer Council
author, The Praying Youth Ministry

PLANNING A PRAYER RETREAT

An Easy Step-By-Step Guide

for

Organizing And Leading
Group Prayer Retreats

DEBORAH J.A. MILLER, ED. D, D. MIN.

Published by KHARIS PUBLISHING, imprint of KHARIS MEDIA LLC.

Copyright © 2025 Deborah J.A. Miller, Ed. D, D. Min.

ISBN-13:978-1-63746-349-9

ISBN-10:1-63746-349-9

Library of Congress Control Number: 2025946178

All rights reserved. This book or parts thereof may not be reproduced in any form, stored in a retrieval system, or transmitted in any form by any means - electronic, mechanical, photocopy, recording, or otherwise - without prior written permission of the publisher, except as provided by United States of America copyright law.

All KHARIS PUBLISHING products are available at special quantity discounts for bulk purchases for sales promotions, premiums, fund-raising, and educational needs. For details, contact:

Kharis Media LLC
Tel: 1-630-909-3405
support@kharispublishing.com
www.kharispublishing.com

Table of Contents

Introduction ix
Why This Guide Book? ix

Chapter One 15
My Personal Prayer Journey 15

Chapter Two 43
A Biblical Case For Corporate Prayer 43

Chapter Three 54
Who Goes On A Prayer Retreat? 54

Chapter Four 69
What Exactly Is A Prayer Retreat? 69

Chapter Five 77
Where And When Should Group Prayer Retreats Occur? 77

Chapter Six 84
The Prayer Retreat Flow 84

Chapter Seven 107
After The Event 107

Chapter Eight 114
Stuff To Think About 114

Chapter Nine 128
Conclusion 128

Appendix A *133*

Appendix B *143*

Bibliography.. *147*

INTRODUCTION
WHY THIS GUIDE BOOK?

> Almighty God, you have given us grace at this time with one accord to make our common supplication to you; and you have promised through your well beloved Son that when two or three are gathered together in his Name you will be in the midst of them: Fulfill now, O Lord, our desires and petitions as may be best for us; granting us in this world knowledge of truth, and in the age to come life everlasting. Amen.
> —A Prayer of St. John Chrysostom

I've been "doing" prayer for a long time. By that I mean I've been talking to God ever since I was a child—and that is certainly the simplest definition of prayer. Sometimes that talking looked like singing, or crying, or complaining. It sometimes looked like listening, and thinking hard about His Word, or pondering His commands, all in a posture of receptivity to the voice of the Holy Spirit. It has meant thanking Him with profound gratitude in awe and wonder at His goodness. It has meant being boringly repetitious because, well, I was just going through the motions, not from a place of indifference or hardness of heart, but mostly due to exhaustion. I heard a saying once that so simply characterizes our prayer lives sometimes: "Anything worth doing is worth doing poorly."[1] I am thankful for the wisdom of these words that gave me grace to practice the discipline of prayer even when I had very little to offer God by way of energy and attention. (Any mothers of young children know what I'm talking about here.)

My identity as a person who prays has spanned the years, from a young child talking to a God I hardly knew, (but wanted to!); through teen angst; to the prayers of a newly married woman; then as a young mom; to the prayers of a woman balancing career, home, and family; and to more complex and intimate times of communion with a God I have come to know much more deeply as the decades have passed, a God I have come to trust, to rely upon, to love from the depths of my being.

I believe we were made for God, and that our deepest longings are only satisfied in communion with Him. Our joy and deep contentment as human beings are directly proportional to the level of our intimacy with the One who made us. When our lives are rooted and grounded in our relationship with Him—purpose, meaning, vision, direction—LIFE flows in and through

---

[1] This quotation has been attributed to G.K. Chesterton, though I first heard it in a Multnomah University chapel message given by Dr. Garry Friesen.

us. And this relationship is fundamentally dependent on His communication with us and our communication with Him. That is prayer.

As I will explain shortly, my journey as a believer is marked by my journey as a pray-er. I have grown closer to God as I have learned to pray. E.M. Bounds said, "Those who know God the best are the richest and most powerful in prayer."[2] I agree with him, and would add that one of the most profound ways to know Him is to spend time with Him in prayer—in all of its forms and variations. Often my times of prayer have been a solo adventure. However, some of the most intense and meaningful prayer times I have had have been in communion with others as we sought God together in prayers of agreement, in joint worship, in intercessory prayer for each other and others. Sometimes these group prayer sessions occurred on prayer retreats where I was able to spend prolonged times in guided prayer with others.

Because prayer retreats have been so valuable in my own development as a child of God, and because I have been able to facilitate meaningful prayer retreats for others so they could experience the same transformational impact, I felt it was time to make available the blueprint for a prayer retreat so that others could taste the fruit of such an experience.

---

[2] E. M. Bounds, *Prayer and Praying Men* (Grand Rapids, MI: Baker Books, 1977), 45.

Planning a Prayer Retreat

I am convinced one of the reasons that group prayer retreats are not very common is that people aren't really sure what to do. I am also convinced it is not *mainly* about details regarding logistics, or registration, or how to plan meals, though those are very important and can be daunting, and will be covered in this Guidebook. The single greatest barrier to seeing prayer retreats normalized as a part of what the body of Christ does when we want to spend an extended time seeking God together is simply knowing how to build out an experience of prayer that is life giving, meaningful to everyone who shows up. What does one *do*? Or more accurately, what does the group do? This Guidebook will lay out all the essential components, including an agenda or schedule of actions that outlines how to create that experience. This retreat agenda will create a rhythm of waiting, listening, moving, interceding, strategizing—all of it—that moves without driving, demanding, or pushing. It is invitational. It carries expectations for engagement, but with joyful eagerness to hear God speak and see Him move. What does the Word say? *"For where two or three are gathered together in my name, I am there in the midst of them."*[3] and *"…in your presence is fullness of joy…,"*[4] and, *"Now the Lord is the Spirit; and where the Spirit of the Lord is, there is liberty."*[5]

---

[3] Matthew 18:20 (NKJV)
[4] See Psalm 16:11 (NKJV)
[5] 2 Corinthians 3:17 (NKJV)

Deborah J. A. Miller, ED. D, D. MIN.

When we gather to pray, He comes into our space as the Holy Spirit, and brings a fullness of God-sourced joy and freedom. He brings direction, vision, unity, perspective, hope, and inspiration. Can I get an "Amen"? Who wouldn't want to be a part of that experience? It's within your reach – simple, though perhaps not easy. Doable, but not without embracing the essential parts that will be shared; it's reproduceable, if you pay attention to the details and realize that each step of the process or agenda, in the order given, creates and builds out the full experience.

My desire for this short Guidebook is this: I hope and pray that my story and the time-tested structure and advice gained from experience will serve the reader in planning and implementing prayer retreats—retreats that can change the trajectory of your own personal prayer life and the lives of others for whom you make this opportunity available. I believe God will grant you the same blessing of His transformational presence as you intentionally engage in a group prayer retreat with your church, friends, or whomever God puts on your heart to join you!

CHAPTER ONE

MY PERSONAL PRAYER JOURNEY

> "Praying together is not a luxury, nor is it something just for 'spiritual' Christians; it's the very breath of the church. Most of us don't have the faintest idea of what that means."
> —**Paul E. Miller,** *A Praying Church, Becoming a People of Hope in a Discouraging World.* (Wheaton: Crossway, 2023) 7.

I want to start this Guidebook by sharing my testimony of coming to faith in Christ and then my personal prayer journey. I want to begin this way because I think it's good to testify to the goodness of God in drawing us to Him, as well as showing you that I have earned my *bonafides* to write this Guidebook in the prayer school of hard knocks. In other words, I'm no super Christian. Though I have matured in my

Christian walk, I have had the regular struggles and challenges that we call "life." Like you, perhaps, my path has had its twists and turns, potholes and full-blown washouts. Of course, every mile of the adventure on Planet Earth has provided the opportunity to pray; thus my prayer life has been constantly under construction. I've learned from some amazing mentors, and I've developed some skill, if I can say that. I have learned about prayer from studying God's Word, reading *a lot* about it (three years of grad school and a dissertation on prayer equated to about ten thousand pages of reading and writing, give or take a few), and practicing it (with varying degrees of success).

Yet even with all those beautiful and amazing inputs, intimacy with God through prayer still takes effort and discipline; I have to be diligent to fan the flames of my first love so that I am passionate in my pursuit of God in prayer. I share this so that wherever you are in your own prayer life development, you can be encouraged that having a fruitful prayer life is within your grasp. I know that for a fact. Simply to want to learn to pray is a step in the right direction. That you are reading this book is proof of your desire—a desire that God will honor. If you want to develop a deeper prayer life, this Guidebook will help you. Be excited! So, let me share with you a bit of my past, so you can get to know me a little and see that God can teach us regular Janes and Joes how to be effectual and fervent in our prayer lives, that our prayers "might avail much."[6]

I accepted Christ as my Savior at a Vacation Bible School when I was twelve. It happened sort of by accident. It was a warm June day and I and a half-dozen or so other pre-teen compadres were being held captive in the basement of centuries-old Hillside Bible Church, a little country church nestled in the foothills of the Coast Range in a western Oregon hamlet. We were (sort of) listening to the well-meaning, soft-spoken pastor's wife explain the message of the Gospel. To be honest, it was something probably all of us had heard before, so none of us were listening with wide-eyed wonder. I think most of us were simply enduring the lesson, just hoping for it to be done so we could go outside. With half an ear, I heard what sounded like the lead-in to a wrap up, so I turned my full attention to the teacher's words. She asked, "So, is there anyone who would like to pray a prayer of salvation, inviting Jesus to be the Lord of your life?" We all shot sideways glances at each other to see if anyone's hand would go up. *Please*, I thought, *someone put us out of our misery*. Somehow, I knew we weren't leaving until she had seen some fruit from her earnest pleas. The crowd sat silently. The teacher waited. She again invited us to consider taking this important step, followed by a lengthy pause. *Great*, I thought, *we're never getting out of here until someone caves*. At that moment, I took a

---

[6] James 5:16b (NKJV)

calculated risk, considering that if I stuck up my hand, and followed her in a (short, I hoped) responsive prayer, I would be the hero for the day, releasing myself and the rest of the gang to the great outdoors and out of the stuffy confines of the concrete basement. With a surge of martyr-level adrenalin, my arm shot up; my eyes looked up as well, to be sure she saw my sacrificial hand. Seeing my response, the teacher's face broke into a smile of delight, and then the moment took an unforeseen turn. She looked at the rest of the class and said, "Well, the rest of you are released to break while, Deborah, I want you to stay here with me during the free time so we can pray and discuss what it means to be a follower of Jesus." *WHAT? Unexpected twist and epic backfire.* I was stunned and dismayed. While I admittedly saw the value of becoming a Christian, I most definitely did not want to spend my entire break talking about it. *Ugh, it was a sacrifice too great!* At least the rest of the kids were set free, and grateful and sympathetic looks graced me as everyone took off like bats out of…a stifling mid-century church basement. Resigned to my fate, I turned my attention to the sinner's prayer and my twelve-year-old conception of what it meant to make Jesus "Lord."

Figure 1: Historic Hillside Bible Church, Forest Grove, Oregon. Hillside Bible Church website.

I don't remember much more about that moment. I knew, thanks to an extensive conversation on the price Jesus paid and the cost of discipleship, that something eternally significant happened that day. And while it was a bumpy take off, the fruit of my conversion actually began to grow rather quickly. Turns out, junior high school STINKS! (I was actually thinking of a different word, but I'm trying to use self-control.) The two years that followed were brutal in terms of bullying, social awkwardness, nightmares like that Spring Social where you stand in the wings and never get asked to dance. Please tell me SOMEONE else has experienced that humiliation… it was a rough time of life. I needed Jesus to save me from sin *and* Marci (yes, that was her real name… I'm not protecting her because she wasn't innocent) and her gang. I needed to know I had value and was loved and that there was life outside of torturous school.

The relationship I forged with Christ in those challenging teen years laid a foundation upon which I have built for the last forty-something years. Thankfully, we serve a gracious and understanding God who takes our meager fish and loaves offering and turns it into a banquet. I looked back on that VBS church basement moment with embarrassment for my pre-teen stupidity, but also gratitude for a thirty-something-year-old pastor's wife who labored faithfully to share the Gospel with someone as clueless and thankless as myself. I will never forget that day, or, more accurately, the outcome of the commitment I made that day. I look forward to a moment in eternity when I will be able to express a proper "thank you" to a woman whose name I can't even remember. I believe I'll know it then, and it will be an honor and privilege to offer her my profound gratitude for persisting in calling a roomful of yahoo's to salvation. I am a life who was changed.

I begin my prayer story there because, despite the ignoble beginning, that prayer for salvation turned into earnest and real prayer in my life. My middle-school self-cried out regularly to God. My high-school self-found a way to drive myself eight miles from our home in the tulies to a church in town, to seek a relationship with the pastor's wife who taught the high school Sunday school class.

Each Sunday, she would ask us how we saw God move in our lives during the past week. As a lowly 9th grader, I kept my peace. But always having a tender heart for the hurting, I agonized for the teacher over the lack of responses, week after week, after week. And by "lack of responses," I mean no one had anything to say. Every week the group endured that awkward moment where she posed the question and everyone sat staring at the walls, or the floor, or their hands, or...wherever, with never a voice raised. Yet, she never stopped asking (What is it with the persistence of pastors' wives?). Looking back, I can't bring myself to believe that no one actually saw God move, but maybe that was the reality of the situation. More likely, no one wanted to appear too spiritual or risk suggesting they were seeing God move, only to find they were the only ones. So, I took another calculated risk (of course, at the time, I made no connection to my VBS experience that backfired in the most spectacularly positive way). I found myself determined to look for signs that God was on the move so I would have something to say the following Sunday. Of course, not so shockingly, when we look for signs of God's movement in our lives, we will see it, because He is constantly speaking, moving, and revealing Himself to us if we are paying attention. And I was! That next Sunday, the teacher started with the same inevitable question, but this time, someone responded - I did! I shared, haltingly, with great trepidation, how I thought I'd seen God move. Some of the other students looked at me like I was from another planet. Some looked surprised and even admiringly. But Danna, the teacher ... she looked...happy. Radiant. The risk I took was a very small price to pay to see the joy on her face, and that began a relationship that lasted for years.

THE VALUE OF PRAYER MENTORS

Over the next few years until I went to college, Danna became my prayer mentor (the first of two I've been privileged to know). Many Saturdays, I would go to her house to bake bread. In reality, the bread making was just a subterfuge (yes, we DID make delicious bread, but that's not why I went) so that I could spend the morning praying with her and her daughters. What a gift I received to sit around the small kitchen table

Planning a Prayer Retreat

with three godly women and pray as we waited for the bread to rise. This was my first experience with group prayer beyond just bowing my head as someone prayed an opening prayer at church. The many lessons I learned during that season of life had an immeasurable impact on me as a Christian, but specifically as a praying Christian. Danna taught me to pray with authority as a child of God; she prayed as someone who had a deep personal relationship with a real heavenly Father. Never mind we couldn't see Him; her confidence was unflagging and absolute that His Spirit was present, and He was listening as we bowed our heads and sought His face. Her belief that our prayers could see His kingdom come and His will be done was nothing less than transformational in my understanding of God and my willingness to approach the throne of grace with confidence.

Danna's prayers were relational and confident, spanning a wide range of topics. I learned there is nothing too big or small to take to the Lord in prayer. I also learned that prayer was not dependent on time, place, or posture. We moved from the table to the kitchen counter to check the rising dough and back to the table without having to formally end prayer time so we could move in and out of our "seated with hands folded and heads bowed" position. We prayed as we went. It varied in intensity, but I realized that prayer was a state of mind and heart, not conditioned on a posture, or a certain setting or set of conditions. My prayer life today has grown from seeds planted during those teen years, and I'm eternally grateful to the Lord and to Danna for those precious Saturday mornings.

Danna was not my only prayer mentor. I had the additional blessing of another woman of God that He allowed my path to cross in my journey as a praying woman. During my young adult years, my husband and I attended a church that also ran a Christian school, where I taught English. When I started having babies, I cut back to part time, so I looked for someone who could watch first one and then two children during the time I was teaching. That led me to Cindy, a lady in our church who did in-home childcare for a small number of children. She graciously agreed to take on Grant first, and eventually, Melissa. From the moment she first began watching Grant, it was just WOW. I had not only won the childcare jackpot, but also found another prayer warrior to teach and inspire me. When we each recognized our affinity for prayer, we decided to pray together once a week when I came to pick up the kids. Again, what a gift to me, as I learned from her how to pray the Scriptures, how to proclaim God's Word with authority during intercession.

Cindy taught me prevailing prayer. She became a dear friend and prayer warrior on whom I relied when I had needs that required fervent prayer. One of those times I'll share as both a quasi-comical and as a testimony to her vibrant, bold prayer life. The day I went into labor with my daughter, November 8, 1989, started as normal as a day can start when you are ten months pregnant and could go into labor at any moment. When my contractions started, my husband and I made our way to the hospital, where I was admitted and entered the process of having that baby. An early examination showed the baby was in distress; the concerned look of the doctor told me it could be serious. A trauma team was ready as she made her entrance into the world and was immediately whisked away for examination. As the minutes passed, we got updates: the nurses couldn't get her body temperature up to normal range. Concerned about underlying issues, they drew her blood; the report came to us later that it was the consistency of pink lemonade. From there, they decided she needed to be taken by ambulance to a neonatal intensive care unit in the "big city," so she was kept in an incubator until the ambulance could arrive. I was able to hold her little hand through the plastic sleeve. Roger and I prayed; our hearts were in fear for the unknown.

When the transport team arrived, a doctor came in to see us. His news was basically all bad. Blood tests revealed there was a hole in the umbilical cord...she'd been living off her red blood cells for oxygen and her blood sugar for nourishment...one hour from being stillborn...her prognosis? Oxygen deprivation could have resulted in brain damage; eyes and ears not functioning at full capacity; cerebral palsy...I think I stopped listening after that, unable to take any more in. To top it off, there was no room at the destination hospital for me, so I would not be able to go with her. Roger and my sister Suzie followed the ambulance to that hospital; the team transfused our baby during transport and again upon arrival. Meanwhile, back in my lonely hospital room, I lay numb, anxious and exhausted. What could I do?

I immediately sensed some direction from the Lord. I called Cindy, who drove to the hospital immediately. She came into my room, dropped her coat and purse on the nearest surface, and "reported for duty." I don't know how much life-and-death-storm-the-gates-of-heaven kind of praying you've done, but it's a real thing, and it is not for the faint of heart. When Cindy arrived at my room around 9:00 pm, I briefly updated her, and thus began almost three hours of intercession that included pacing (Cindy, not me…I was confined to the bed), hands raised, all kinds of very loud, insistent crying out to God. The hospital staff would open the door, assess what was happening, and then either quickly do their business while the praying continued, or, in the case of one nurse, simply assess the situation and back themselves out of the room as quickly as they came in. I was too desperate to be embarrassed; looking back, I can only

> "God is not aloof. He says continually through the centuries, 'I'll help you. I really will. When you're ready to throw up your hands—throw them up to me.'"
> —Jim Cymbala, *Fresh Wind, Fresh Fire* (Grand Rapids, MI: Zondervan, 2018) 57.

imagine the conversations at the nurses' desk! When I was no longer able to keep my eyes open, we agreed that we had "prayed it through" and Cindy went home. The next day I got up, checked myself out of the hospital and drove to OHSU in Portland, Oregon, where Roger and I and various visitors stood vigil through the long hours. After a few days, with her health still hanging in the balance, I went home exhausted, only to awaken in the middle of the night with an overwhelming sense of dread. I began to do spiritual warfare, but I was weary to the bone and had little left in the way of energy, hope, or even faith; yet, God. He gave me the very words to pray that I remember to this day, and have prayed over others as well: "God, please heal Melissa to whatever extent she needs to be healed to fulfill your purposes for her life." And with that, peace invaded the darkness, and I was able to sleep.

The reality is that thousands of prayers for healing have been prayed where little or no physical healing occurs. And yet my faith demands that I obey God's Word to *"continue steadfastly in prayer"*[7] and *"In everything by prayer and supplication, with thanksgiving" to let my requests be made known to God.*[8] So, I pray, and like millions of other Christ followers throughout the ages, I trust that the God Who is Love will respond according to His highest glory and for my greatest

---

[7] Romans 12:12(NKJV).
[8] Philippians 4:6-7(NKJV).

good. It's not easy to hold that position or belief in the face of incredible human suffering, but it is essential that we believers honor, trust, and respect a sovereign God's right to be our sovereign God.

In the days that followed, we got miracle report after miracle report. Further tests revealed no brain damage, no organ damage, no muscle damage. Melissa was released from the neonatal care unit a week later with a clean bill of health. I will forever be indebted to all those who prayed for Missy, while being firmly convinced that deep, kingdom-impacting, essential-to-Melissa's-life intercessory work happened in my hospital room that first night with Cindy. For years after Missy's birth, Cindy continued to care for her and her brother until they were of school age. And we continued to pray. Words cannot do justice to the treasures Cindy imparted to me as a prayer mentor, a surrogate mother to my children, and as my friend. She is another for whom I am forever grateful.

A CHURCH WITH ROBUST CORPORATE PRAYER

As you can see, I have had the privilege of two powerful prayer mentors in my life. I also have experienced the impact of the church we were attending at that season of our lives, a church that had a strong commitment, starting with the pastor and his staff, to corporate prayer.[9] Far beyond just lip service to the value of prayer, the leadership established a culture of prayer through creating a framework of corporate prayer practices, expecting staff leaders to attend as a part of their responsibilities, as well as being part of the expectations for those serving in lay leadership at this church. Thankfully, the responsibility to engage in corporate prayer was embraced by leaders—both paid staff and laity alike—which gave strong support and influenced buy-in throughout the congregation.

Let me share about just two of these prayer times. First, the church had pre-service prayer in a fellowship room that could hold at least one hundred people, directly across the hall from the sanctuary. Here, thirty minutes before the service, pastors, staff, lay leaders, volunteers, and anyone else would gather to pray for the service. Individuals would sit or stand or pace and intercede for the church service or anything else for which they felt led to pray. The room was filled with a cacophony of voices lifted to the Lord. At times, someone would step forward with a call to agree together in prayer, or to read a passage, or to share a word they believed the Lord had given for that time.

---

[9] "Corporate prayer" as used in this book refers to members of the body of Christ joining together in a spirit of unity and agreement to worship, intercede, petition, or in any other form communicate with God. This is more than individuals in proximity having their own personal prayer time. It means that there is a unified expression where the body is expressing itself to God in agreement and shared purpose.

When time came for the service, the masses would migrate across the foyer into the sanctuary, carrying with them a palpable sense of expectation and excitement.

Along with those weekly pre-service prayer times, the church also held a week of prayer and fasting each year. Every night during that week, members would gather for prayer for a couple of hours. The depth of those prayer times, enriched by fasting, influenced my perception and belief that intense times of prayer were very productive in the spiritual realm, and that prayer, like a muscle, was strengthened and built up by exercise, both consistency at a certain "weight" and pushing the boundaries by asking more of our muscles—even our prayer muscles. This spirit of prayer carried over to leader meetings and almost any other gathering. The ethos of prayer in that community of believers indelibly marked me. I came to be convinced that prayer in all its forms ought to have a preeminent place in the life of the church.

AN EXPERIMENT: Would Students Come Together Just to Pray?

During this season of life as a high school teacher, I led my first overnight student prayer retreat. I thought, *Why not teach young people how amazing times of sustained prayer can be?* So I made a plan, found an affordable venue, and asked God to give me twelve students who would be willing to come away with me for prayer. The Lord gave me a design plan for our time together, which I'll share in a later chapter, and we took that first retreat...and it was glorious. Students didn't know what to expect (Neither did I, really!), but the plan God gave me kept a rhythm and pace that made praying for twelve hours possible. At the conclusion of that retreat, the students and I practically floated out to our cars to head back to school. And this one was no fluke; throughout the years of leading student prayer retreats, I've seen the depth of students' spiritual lives radically impacted as a result of these experiences. In fact, one senior reported in an interview for the year book that the high school experience she would most remember was the prayer retreat.

IF STUDENTS WILL, WHAT ABOUT ADULTS?

Since those first days, I have had the privilege of leading prayer retreats for church leadership groups, for college students, and for women's ministries. Each retreat had its own purpose, flavor, and outcomes. God brought vision, deepened relationships, established unity, brought correction, made room for repentance, and drew people closer to the Lord. While I would say all have been "good," I also have come to realize that the impact of these events can vary, based on the intent and spiritual maturity and hunger of those who choose to go, apart from anything I can do as a leader or facilitator. Additionally, the logistics and attention to detail can have an impact on the success of the event by creating an atmosphere and circumstances that are either more or less conducive to robust prayer.

Not every prayer retreat has been a "**ten**," if we could even all agree what that would look like. For the sake of clarity, I would define a "ten" *not* as a retreat where every detail worked out exactly as planned, every part of the agenda ran smoothly, every meal was on time, or every person was completely happy with the total experience. No, a "ten" for me would be a retreat where all the participants were engaged consistently for the majority of time, where each contributed what he or she had to offer, and where a sweet spirit of unity, fellowship, and willingness to yield to the Holy Spirit characterized the overall experience. Success would definitely require a sense that the Spirit of God was welcome, showed up, and His presence marked the direction and substance of the work of prayer and ministry. Before you take a retreat, it would be valuable for you as the leader to consider what success would look like to you, as it might affect your planning and implementation. As far as the retreats I have led and what success meant to me, I think most have been what I can term successful, but even a time-tested formula is not a guarantee of a mountaintop experience. So I will share what I think helps set up the best opportunity for success and what pitfalls to avoid so we don't give the enemy an opportunity to sidetrack, distract, or bring division on these retreats.

Overwhelmingly, I would say that prayer retreats have had a significant impact on the lives of those in attendance. But the beauty of a prayer retreat is that it not only bears lasting fruit in the lives of those involved, but also has a powerful impact on the recipients of those prayers, whether that means individuals, churches, causes, events, etc. Prayer changes things. The outcomes of prayer retreats are beyond what we can see with our natural eyes, which is why I am such a proponent of them, and why I am writing this book to encourage others to engage in them as well. Here's an example of the impact that one prayer retreat had on a specific organization.

A PRAYER RETREAT I'LL NEVER FORGET

While every prayer retreat I have led has memorable moments and elicits warm recollections, some have been truly Kingdom-changing. One of the most powerful prayer retreats I recall was one I instigated at the prompting of the Holy Spirit on behalf of an organization that had recently hired me. There were some serious internal and external challenges, serious enough to cause widespread, deep concern across the entire organization. In a time of prayer, I believed God urged me to call my counterparts across the USA to a time of prayer, "on our own dime and our own time." A recent hire, I was ambivalent about taking this "word of the Lord" to my superior as a suggested plan of action. We were set to have a private Zoom® call, where I broached the idea with him. He listened, honored my idea by giving it his full support, and offered to let me share the idea on the next directors' zoom call. I had secretly hoped he would just take the idea and run with it, but God had other plans.

So at the next call a few weeks later, with not a little fear and trembling, I gingerly offered up the idea of a prayer retreat. To my surprise (*O me of little faith*) with no hesitation everyone agreed, despite none of them having experienced a prayer retreat like this before. The group collaborated on a plan, set a date, and soon the weekend was upon us. We met in a central location at a house big enough to accommodate us all, and we spent two and a half days seeking God. Again, I used the same template to establish the rhythm and flow, though, of course, each experience is unique to the group and the need. Despite early skepticism (One colleague asked, "We aren't really going to spend all this time actually praying, are we?), the time away was a sacred event for everyone. Although we did not conclude our time together receiving a definitive call to action or some divine declaration from God, we agreed God had heard our prayers and we believed they would be efficacious.

Within weeks, there were major shifts in the organization that came as a great surprise to many. For those of us who attended the retreat, there was less shock and more prayers of gratitude--we believed the changes were due, in no small part, to the time we had spent in intercession. God is real. He tells us to pray, and when we do, He listens and moves. Yes, it is a mystery that has been pondered by thousands and studied and written about by hundreds…why the God of the universe expects us to pray and chooses to listen and respond. And it is true that some who have studied this mystery conclude that the God of the Universe does not respond to our prayers through external, tangible acts; that He simply wants to shape *us* through the process of our prayers. But I and many others believe that God, though He need not, has chosen to invite us to make requests of Him, requests that, when they are according to His will, He not only hears but to which He responds.[10] This belief is not only supported by the story I've shared here, but also by thousands of other testimonies of believers and promises in Scripture.

Praying, individually and together, is commanded, modeled, and taught in Scripture, as we will see in the next chapter. We may not fully understand the dynamics of prayer because it isn't formulaic: God isn't a vending machine into which we put prayer coins in order to see the answer we want dispensed. Because prayer isn't transactional, but dynamic and relational, God is not forced to give us what we ask. Sometimes He says, "No," or "Wait," or simply nothing at all. He is Sovereign over the affairs of humankind, and when we come to Him in prayer, it is with humble submission and recognition of the fact that we ought not to make

---

[10] I John 5:14-15 states, *"And this is the confidence that we have in him, that if we ask anything according to his will, he hears us. And if we know that he hears us—whatever we ask—we know that we have what we asked of him."*

demands of Him like spoiled children, stamping our feet and shaking our fists, and thinking we can tire Him out through endless repetition. We humbly make our requests and trust Him to work His perfect will as He chooses to respond to our petitions. If we are coming to Him in prayer out of simple obedience, it's well and good. If we have faith that can move mountains, that's even better. What is important is that we come—alone in our prayer closets or as groups of believers—to seek His face, to cry out, to make intercession. When people come together to seek God's face like this, history is changed. Prayer retreats, as one form of coming *en masse*, are incredibly powerful in the lives of believers and the churches, organizations, causes, and needs for which they pray. I hope you are beginning to catch a vision of just how significant these kinds of prayer events can be!

As that organization found its footing again, and returned to thriving, it invited me to lead a team to develop international days of prayer for their global network. Working together, we were able to connect thousands of schools around the world on behalf of tens of thousands of children in days of prayer. While I am no longer with this organization, the worldwide day of prayer is still happening, joining Christians across the globe. What amazing fruit can come when we obediently follow the call of God to invite others to prayer.

LAST, BUT DEFINITELY NOT LEAST: *A Pillar of Prayer in My Life*

It may seem odd to share about the influence and importance of the prayer time I have with my spouse. Does praying with one other person constitute corporate prayer? Well, technically, yes! There are many resources on the benefits of a prayer partner, and I strongly recommend you explore that topic if you are at all interested. Prayer partners are valuable for a number of reasons: accountability, support, and deep friendship, to name a few. And when your prayer partner is also your life partner, the fruit is even sweeter. Given that reality, I would be remiss not to share what is certainly the longest-lasting prayer relationship I have had in my life, and that is with my husband Roger. We have undertaken some big exploits in our lives, fully aware as we embarked upon them that we were never going to be able to accomplish anything without the presence and power of God leading in every way. Desperation is a very effective motivator to pray!

I won't claim that we have spent time in prayer together every day since we've been married. That would most certainly not be true. Even after we had established a routine of daily prayer in a season of deep need, we had seasons of droughts where we let those times lapse. Some of those droughts lasted a few years. Thankfully, we realized the need to restore the daily discipline of prayer together as necessary for the health of our relationship and the benefit of our family, so I'm happy to say that we now rarely miss a day and haven't for well over a decade. Our habit now is to arise each morning, get our coffee, and settle into our prayer chairs for at least thirty minutes of prayer.

Sometimes we come to prayer out of sheer discipline and not eager anticipation. However we get to prayer, God always meets us there. Honestly, this time is not always spectacular; we don't sense every day that we've done groundbreaking work in our intercession. However, many days seem very spiritually productive; God leads us by His Holy Spirit into areas of prayer neither of us anticipated, or to pray in ways that are clearly Holy Spirit inspired and not of us. On several occasions we have been led to pray something seemingly random, only to see the very same issue as a headline in the day's news. We come to a topic, and it consumes us for the half hour that we pray. We hear what is in each other's hearts, a wonderful insight for spouses. We leave feeling connected on a spiritual level. I am very thankful for a husband who partners with me in prayer, and I would highly recommend a daily or at least regular time of praying together for every couple. Yes, it takes effort to carve out and then guard the time, but it is well worth it.

FORMALIZING MY ONGOING INTEREST IN PRAYER

As I experienced ebbs and flows in my prayer life over the decades, I came to a season almost three years ago when I decided to invest more time and energy into the topic of prayer. I had just started a doctorate in Ministry in Spiritual Formation and Discipleship at Nazarene Theological Seminary, and in the first term we were pressed to choose a topic for our dissertations. I cast around for a topic that I wanted to dominate my reading, thinking, and writing for three years. It dawned on me that the topic could be corporate prayer. I was giddy with the thought that I could engage deeply in something for which I had a passion (if you have done a doctorate, you know that a rule of thumb for choosing a dissertation topic is to pick something you can *care about* for the months and years it takes you to finish!). And so it began—thousands of pages read, hundreds of pages written on the topic of prayer, and specifically corporate prayer. I can say I am more passionate about it today than I was when I started. I am convinced that prayer is the most important spiritual discipline in the life of a Christ follower, especially given that my definition of prayer is simply any communication with God: confession, repentance, praise, thanksgiving, lament, listening, intercession, petition, adoration, worship, reflection, meditation...*if we are communicating, we are praying.* Like Jesus' disciples, I will be a student of prayer perhaps throughout eternity, unless somehow we gain all knowledge and wisdom upon entrance to heaven. But for sure until then, at the least, I will be striving to engage in, as my friend and prayer guru Rev. Dennis Fuqua puts it, "more and better prayer."[11] If I've learned anything in the last few years of studying this topic deeply, a lot of Christians feel a lot of guilt about not having effective prayer lives—*any* prayer life. Even church leaders struggle, knowing it is important, but feeling ineffective and unmotivated to develop more robust prayer lives. I get that. I empathize with those who struggle to initiate or maintain consistent personal times of prayer, because I recognize prayer is a discipline. Notice I did not say a personal time of "devotions." Surely like many others, I have a daily time reading my Bible, contemplating its truths, and journaling my insights, and certainly there is an element of communing with the Spirit during that time. To be frank, though, engaging in prayer for myself or others takes more discipline, more planning, and more effort. I am more disciplined than I used to be. I have found ways to stay focused in prayer, to train my thoughts. I have discovered some amazing apps, some liturgical tools, and other supports that continue to enrich and develop my personal prayer time. But the fuel that keeps my prayer tank topped-off is all the

---

[11] I highly encourage readers to explore *United and Ignited Encountering God through Dynamic Corporate Prayer* by Dennis Fuqua (Vancouver, WA: L/P Press), 2012) for great insights and practical advice on facilitating corporate prayer.

Planning a Prayer Retreat

times that I engage with others for prolonged times of prayer.

I absolutely believe we need to have personal times of prayer when we are alone in communion with the Creator, but I also absolutely believe that corporate body life, including prayer, is not a secondary or inferior form of prayer. I believe He wants us to pray together as much as He wants us to pray on our own. Jesus declared, *"My Father's house shall be a house of prayer..."*[12] Not teaching, though we know that is essential. Not fellowship, not service, not giving, although we know all those are essential. No, we are to be houses of *prayer* for the nations. Even the disciples realized the great importance of prayer. The ONE thing Jesus' disciples asked Him to teach them, most of whom were raised in synagogues where prayer happened frequently, was how to pray. Jesus' response was to teach them what we now refer to as "The Lord's Prayer"[13] —notably, a prayer to be prayed together. Prayer really, really matters. Our churches need to recover an emphasis on corporate prayer! The opportunity to spend intensive, prolonged time with others seeking the face of God is a profound way to shape our prayer lives.

I do not believe prayer is a spiritual gift or calling that some believers have. Prayer is something we all must do and can do. Prayer by ourselves and with

---

[12] Isaiah 56:7
[13] Matthew 6:5-15

others is a practice that will continue throughout eternity in some form or fashion, since we will never cease to worship, praise, or give thanks. I do not know what the role of intercession or lament or confession will be in heaven, but if there will be no sorrow there, then perhaps those types of prayer will have no place. Yet, we will still experience rich communion with the Father, Son, and Holy Spirit. Now is the time to learn and lean in to the many ways we can commune with Him in prayer.

HOW THIS GUIDEBOOK IS ORGANIZED

If you are a detail-oriented person, congratulations. I, however, have a love/hate relationship with details. This has been somewhat challenging, given that I have served in multiple leadership roles over the decades, all of which required some attention to the granular. It doesn't come naturally, so I credit the grace of God and good administrative support for helping me to keep all my ducks corralled, if not in neat rows. Because I don't love details, but realize how necessary they are, I have sympathy for other big picture thinkers who would rather dream than wade through a river of necessary but mind-numbing (at least to me) particulars. Because I recognize how easily things fall apart when each jot and tittle has not been addressed, I painstakingly tried to process each element of putting on a group prayer retreat, knowing that attention to the specifics would be a blessing for both the detail lovers and those like me who don't want to have to live in that thinking space more than they have to. I hope I've done the bulk of that kind of thinking for you. For that reason, this Guidebook is laid out in a very straightforward manner, from providing the big picture vision to addressing the nitty-gritty elements that are so vital to fulfill that vision. I have shared my journey so that you now have some background as to why I wrote this book; next, I will lay out a scriptural foundation for corporate prayer, and then I will share all the details of implementing a prayer retreat in a "who, what, where, when, why, how" format so that the information is easy to follow. So, before we launch into the practical material, let's examine the Scriptures to build a biblical rationale for a group prayer retreat.

CHAPTER TWO

A BIBLICAL CASE FOR CORPORATE PRAYER

We may not fully understand the dynamics of prayer because it isn't formulaic: God isn't a vending machine into which we put prayer coins in order to see the answer we want dispensed. Because prayer isn't transactional, but dynamic and relational, God is not forced to give us what we ask.

OLD TESTAMENT SUPPORT FOR CORPORATE PRAYER

Some readers may wish to skip this more academic chapter since it doesn't address the practical "how tos" of running a group prayer retreat. And that is understandable for a number of reasons. Perhaps you already have a strong theology or biblical understanding of corporate prayer. Or perhaps you don't feel a need to examine the biblical case for corporate prayer; you know God likes it when we pray, and that's good enough for you. Or maybe you see the need or value in knowing there is a biblical case for corporate prayer, but are satisfied knowing it exists without needing to revisit it in this moment. Okay; well and good. However, as one early reader pointed out, since I thought it was important to include, it might be valuable for you to read! And I found it valuable to include because of the basic principle that the Bible should be the foundation for everything the Body of Christ does, including how we pray. I found it quite inspirational to see how much the Bible has to say about prayer, including corporate prayer.

Since you've made it this far, I would encourage you to let your faith be built up regarding the Scriptural support for corporate prayer by reading the chapter. There's my rationale—so, you choose: read it and enjoy it; skip it and come back to it if you ever have the desire or need; skip it and never come back to it. If case two or three applies, just know the biblical rationale is here should you ever decide it would be helpful. For the rest of you, let's dive in.

We will begin by examining Old Testament themes and examples of corporate prayer. John Smed illustrates the theme of revival in corporate prayer by pointing out that five national revivals rooted in prayer and repentance occurred during the reigns of Solomon,

Asa, Jehoshaphat, Hezekiah, and Josiah.[14] Another Old Testament theme is the truth that God is present and attentive to the offering of corporate prayers. In 2 Chronicles 7:14-15 (NIV) the Chronicler records God's promise to Solomon as prayers are made in the temple Solomon constructed: *"If my people, who are called by my name, will humble themselves and pray and seek my face and turn from their wicked ways, then I will hear from heaven, and I will forgive their sin and heal their land. Now my eyes will be open and my ears attentive to the prayers offered in this place."* Both the theme of revival and an assurance of God's engaging presence provide current-day impetus to honor the practice of corporate prayer. Examples of corporate prayer in Scripture are noted by several Bible scholars. Dr. Jim Hamilton offers a concise treatment of both Old and New Testament examples of corporate prayer. He writes, "When we look to the OT Writings, we find a great deal on corporate prayer, particularly in the Psalms..."[15] He claims the Psalms were intended to be prayed and sung by God's people as they identify with a righteous covenantal mediator. He points out that other Old Testament examples

---

[14] John Smed, *Prayer Revolution Rebuilding Church and City through Prayer*, (Chicago: Moody Publishers) 2020, 149. For further exploration of this statement, I recommend reading Chapter 8 "How a Nation is Renewed through Repentance," 149-168.

[15] Jim Hamilton, *"A Biblical Theology of Corporate Prayer,"* 9Marks, Feb. 25, 2010, 9marks.org/article/biblical-theology-corporate-prayer/ 1. Hamilton points to Psalm 44 as an example of OT writings written from the perspective of a first-person plural ("we") narrator.

include the Children of Israel crying out when they were oppressed, and calls for corporate prayer in Esther, Ezra, and Nehemiah. Dale Brueggemann provides further examples, drawing attention to the standardized prayers which all Jews were to pray both individually and together, such as the Shema and the Amidah, as well as the corporate prayers and songs uttered in solemn procession, on pilgrimage, or when entering the temple. He also includes Joel's prophetic call to the priests to make intercession together.[16] These examples reveal that corporate prayer was baked into religious practice for both laypeople and priests. Along with the themes and examples of corporate prayer seen in the Old Testament, the New Testament also provides support for individual and corporate prayer through the life and message of Jesus Christ, the birth of the Church, and in the lives and teachings of New Testament authors.

NEW TESTAMENT EMPHASIS ON PRAYER

As general motivation to engage in prayer, we can also look to the life and words of Jesus Christ and other New Testament voices, who consistently place an emphasis on prayer. Jesus expects us to pray. He said to His followers, *"And when you pray, do not use vain*

---

[16] Dale Brueggemann, *"Corporate Prayer in the Old Testament,"* Sermons by Logos. Accessed July 24, 2024, at https://sermons.logos.com/sermons/345365-corporate-prayer-in-the-old-testament?sso=false.

repetitions, as the heathen do."[17] Mark records this instruction of Jesus: *"And whenever you stand praying, if you have anything against anyone, forgive him, that your Father in heaven may also forgive you your trespasses."*[18] In both these passages, Jesus said *when,* not *if.* Jesus also said, *"Watch and pray so that you will not fall into temptation."*[19] Luke records Jesus' telling of the parable of the persistent widow, *"to show them that they should always pray and not give up."*[20] Jesus not only commanded prayer but also modeled a life of prayer, drawing away for intimate times with the Father, praying with and for His disciples on multiple occasions, even pleading with them to corporately intercede for Him the night He was arrested. The whole of His life was a consistent call to ongoing communication in prayer, bequeathing on His disciples before His Ascension the gift of praying in His name: *"And whatever you ask in My name, that I will do, that the Father may be glorified in the Son. If you ask anything in My name, I will do it..."*[21] Clearly, Jesus expected, wanted, and was encouraging communication with Himself and the Father to continue after His resurrection; and this

> Jesus not only commanded prayer but also modeled a life of prayer.

---

[17] Matt. 6:7 (NKJV).
[18] Mark 11:25 (NKJV).
[19] Matt. 26:41a (NIV).
[20] Luke 18:1 (NIV).
[21] John 14:13-14 (NKJV).

for good, Kingdom-advancing reasons. John Smed says, "Praying, especially praying together, is our means of experiencing the present ascension presence and power of Christ."[22] As individuals who profess to be Christ followers, we must pray because it is a command and expectation of God; it is our response to the heart of God seeking fellowship with His beloved, resulting in, as Smed stated, a felt sense of Christ's presence and power.

Prayer was essential to the creation of the early Church. After Jesus' resurrection, His disciples continued to prioritize prayer. As the first act of obedience, the disciples gathered in the upper room to await the gift of the Holy Spirit—an active waiting as they prayed together: *"These all continued with one accord in prayer and supplication, with the women and Mary the mother of Jesus, and with His brothers."*[23]

The Church was born as a result of corporate prayer. As another New Testament figure whose life provides us an example worthy of emulation, the Apostle Paul gives further evidence of the value of prayer. Paul's writing are filled with references to prayer, indicating the high priority given to prayer in his own life and ministry. Paul instructed the churches in Rome, Ephesus, and Philippi regarding the importance of prayer: *"rejoicing in hope, patient in tribulation, continuing steadfastly in prayer"*[24]; *"And pray in the Spirit on all occasions*

---

[22] Smed, *Prayer Revolution*, 22.
[23] Acts 1:14 (NKJV).
[24] Rom. 12:12 (NKJV).

with all kinds of prayers and requests"[25]; and *"Be anxious for nothing, but in everything by prayer and supplication, with thanksgiving, let your requests be made known to God."* [26] Paul urges Timothy to promote prayer: *"I urge, then, first of all, that petitions, prayers, intercession and thanksgiving be made for all people…"* [27] and instructs the Colossians, *"Continue earnestly in prayer, being vigilant in it with thanksgiving"* [28]; to the Thessalonians he says *"Rejoice always, pray without ceasing, in everything give thanks; for this is the will of God in Christ Jesus for you."* [29] Of course, rejoicing, praying, and giving thanks are all forms of prayer—and, as Paul points out, God's will for us. As we can see from the life and writings of Jesus Christ and the Apostle Paul, if we are not engaged in prayer as an active discipline in our lives, both individually and corporately, we are not fulfilling God's will. P.T. Forsyth says, "The worst sin is prayerlessness."[30] Prayer is the primary means through which we access the gracious work of God in our lives. Our prayerlessness is an act of disobedience that robs

> "The worst sin is prayerlessness."

---

[25] Eph. 6:18 (NIV).
[26] Phil. 4:6 (NKJV).
[27] 1 Tim. 2:1-2 (NIV).
[28] Col. 4:2 (NKJV).
[29] 1 Thess. 5:16-18 (NKJV).
[30] P.T. Forsyth, *The Soul of Prayer*, (Waterford: Cross Reach Publications, 2020), 7.

us of our ability to deepen our relationship with Jesus Christ both individually and corporately.

NEW TESTAMENT EMPHASIS ON CORPORATE PRAYER SPECIFICALLY

Along with extensive support for prayer in general, the New Testament also explicitly encourages corporate prayer, which is especially relevant for the purpose of this Guidebook. Let's consider the support of Jesus' teaching on prayer, then look at the early Church's dependence on corporate prayer as further impetus to encourage us to pray together. We see emphases on *corporate* prayer specifically included in the prayer central to the Christian faith, the Lord's Prayer, which famously begins with "Our Father," implying a corporate voice representing the body of Christ. The phrases "give *us*...lead *us*...deliver *us*..." give evidence that this prayer was taught for the gathered people of God, not an individual's closet prayer.

The continuous practice of corporate prayer is also seen throughout the Book of Acts, which serves as a primer on the importance of corporate prayer. We find the disciples waiting for the Holy Spirit in the upper room, as directed by Jesus, engaging in communal prayer.[31] After the Holy Spirit comes with an empowering anointing and infilling, we see the effects on the early Church: they devoted themselves

---

[31] Acts 1:13-14.

to, among other things, prayer.³² In Acts 3:1 we follow Peter and John to the temple at the hour of prayer. Acts 4:24 tell the story of Peter and John's arrest, followed closely by a church prayer meeting by way of response. In Acts 12 Peter is delivered as the church prays. The commissioning of Barnabas and Saul to take the Gospel to the Gentiles comes as a divine directive as the church prays.³³ God directs the church to appoint elders as they are praying in Acts 14:23; when Paul and his team arrive in Philippi, they seek out God-fearing people to pray with them.³⁴ When Paul is departing from Ephesus, he takes time to pray with the believers there,³⁵ behavior he repeated when he and his team departed from Tyre as reported in Acts 21:5-6.

> "For where two or three are gathered together in My name, I am there in the midst of them."
> Matthew 18:20 (NKJV)

In the New Testament, corporate prayer just happened, all the time, everywhere; great needs demanded a great move of God provoking a united effort to cry out for His presence and His intervention. As mentioned, the Church was born out of a period of corporate prayer. Additionally, the exponential growth

---

[32] Acts 2:42.
[33] Acts 13:1-3.
[34] Acts 16:13-16.
[35] Acts 20:36.

and power of the early Church can be attributed in part to the ubiquitousness of their corporate prayer life. Beyond the examples provided through the Book of Acts, we hear Jesus promising, *"For where two or three are gathered together in my name, I am there in the midst of them"*[36]— a verse widely used to advocate for corporate prayer.

Elsewhere in the New Testament, "Paul states regulations for the behavior of men and women in corporate prayer in 1 Corinthians 11 and 14, and he asks the Romans, Ephesians, Philippians, Colossians, and Thessalonians to pray for his ministry.[37] Sue Curran writes, "The first work of the Kingdom is prayer. The early Church made prayer their priority. Their prayer lives dictated their lifestyle so that they might accomplish the Word of God."[38] The early Church prayed together as a response to crisis but also as a part of the rhythm of their spiritual lives.

As you can see from this quick summary of what the Bible has to say about prayer, and specifically corporate prayer, it really is true that God wants us to pray, and to pray together. While this Chapter may not scratch the itch of "applicability," I hope that it encourages you in your own personal prayer journey,

---

[36] Matt. 18:20 (NKJV).

[37] This summary of prayer activity in the book of Acts comes from Hamilton, "A Biblical Theology," 1.

[38] Sue Curran, The Praying Church, Principles & Power of Corporate Praying. (Lake Mary, FL: Creation House Press. 2001) 38.

and as you seek to create opportunities for others to pray together—like, for example, on a prayer retreat! Christians operate best when we act from first principles found in Scripture. So let this overview of support for prayer in the Old and New Testaments strengthen your conviction of the necessity and importance of prayer, both for individuals and for the body of Christ. Now it's time to get on to the "everything you ever needed to know to lead a prayer retreat" part of the book—most likely, the part you've been waiting for. Are you ready? Let's go!

CHAPTER THREE

WHO GOES ON A PRAYER RETREAT?

> "...we have far too little understanding of the place that intercession (as distinguished from prayer for ourselves) ought to have in the Church and the Christian life."
> —**Andrew Murray**, *The Ministry of Intercessory Prayer*. (Minneapolis: Bethany House Publishers, 1981) 13.

Before you even cracked this book open, you may have asked yourself, "Who goes on a prayer retreat?" Like many people, you may wonder, "Aren't prayer retreats for, like, monks and nuns? Or super confused, desperate people?" (Um, yes to all of those scenarios…but wait, there's more.) Perhaps you can imagine monasteries where people seek refuge or a time to be alone with the Lord, more of a personal time of prayer and reflection, but have a hard time imagining a *group* of people getting away to do something similar. I get it—there is not a lot you would find if you did a web search of "group prayer retreats," other than locations where you could pay to go hold an event. Interestingly, if you were searching for information on taking a personal prayer retreat, you would find several dozen resources to direct your experience, from locations to possible agendas, to articles touting their benefits. But the resources are slim to none on holding group prayer retreats. The whys and wherefores, like whether or not you should eat on your prayer retreat or what the schedule could be like, is not information readily available at the touch of your fingertips across a keyboard.

So here is a simple answer to the natural question of who should go on a prayer retreat: any group of people who would like to seek the Lord together for any purpose. For example, I have led prayer retreats for high school students, church leadership teams, for a tier of directors for a major Christian organization, and for a women's ministry leadership team—very different groups with different purposes, needs, and areas of responsibility. Yet each retreat was powerful in the personal lives of the attendees, as well as having an impact on the organizations these people represented.

WHO LEADS A GROUP PRAYER RETREAT?

The key to a successful group prayer retreat starts with a point person—the most important "who" in terms of having an event—someone who sees the value of a prayer retreat and believes it will be of benefit to his or her ministry. This is typically someone in a leadership position or someone who has the support of a leader who can 1) promote the idea of a prayer retreat, 2) get buy-in from those who will be invited to go, or 3) in the case of an open-invitation event, influence a core of people to go. Beyond these simple requirements, I would add these as qualifications for someone leading a prayer retreat: 1) You should have a consistent, active prayer life, both in your individual life ("prayer closet" personal time— which could be your car, your walking trail, your kitchen table, or your actual closet!) and a public prayer life (you confidently pray in public, you might serve on the prayer team, you might be part of the intercessory prayer group, you attend prayer meetings/events); 2) You have a level of spiritual maturity that is affirmed by your pastor or someone from the pastoral team; 3) You have leadership skills in organization and planning; 4) You are known as a person who consistently demonstrates the fruit of the Spirit.[39] This last attribute is most strongly reflected by the health of your human

---

[39] Galatians 5:22.

relationships—if your life produces love, joy, peace, patience, kindness, goodness, faithfulness, gentleness, and self-control, most of your relationships should be healthy and positive.

With these qualifications in mind, if you are a leader who could spearhead a prayer retreat, then following this path is wise: share the idea with your team, tell them why you want to do it, get buy-in from a majority, and then move forward with planning the logistics of the event. If you are not the leader, but simply a member of a team, and God has spoken to you about the need for your team to have a prolonged time of intercessory prayer, then talk to your leader, explain your idea, and trust that God will confirm the need for a retreat if indeed He has spoken to you. With the support of your leader, you can then move ahead with the planning and implementation of your prayer retreat.

Alternatively, you may be like my friend Melissa, who recently just wanted to gather with a group of friends for a day of prayer, and wanted someone who knew what to do to come and facilitate it. Like I did, you can take this Guidebook and use it to equip you to serve as a facilitator for people who might want to hold a prayer retreat. God will meet with whoever you gather to encounter Him in prayer, whether this is a formal ministry team, an organization, extended family, or group of dear friends. Anyone can benefit from a group prayer retreat as long as there is someone there to guide the way.

ATTENDANCE: VOLUNTARY OR MANDATORY? IT DEPENDS...

First, there are many occasions when taking a prayer retreat is an open invitation to anyone who would like to experience an intensive group prayer event. In such cases, once the idea is advertised and signups begin, you want a minimum of eight to ten people to sign up in order to have critical mass. The format that I have used works best if you can recruit eight to ten people at a minimum, because this allows for groups of three to four people in each breakout prayer group, which is optimal for the small group prayer times. While it can be done, neither less than three nor more than four is optimal. Small group prayer in just pairs praying together gets exhausting because two people bear the burden of all the praying. On the other hand, with more than four in a small group prayer time, attention and focus can wander because the group is so big that those in the group won't be praying as much, making it harder to get and keep everyone in the prayer flow for twenty-five minutes at a time.

If the purpose of the prayer retreat is for a specific group to engage in prayer, say for a specific ministry or cause, the numbers guidelines still hold: a minimum of eight to ten people is the target for a successful prayer retreat using the model that I'm going to share. If you have fewer than eight, a prayer retreat can still happen, but the format will need to be modified so individuals don't leave exhausted or frustrated, especially if this is the first time that participants have experienced a prayer retreat.

Groups can certainly be larger than ten, but as the head facilitator, if you have more than twenty-four in attendance you will still want to keep small group prayer time to groups of three or four. With a group larger than twenty-four, during the large group prayer times consider chunking the attendees into groups of twelve to fifteen and having additional facilitators walk the groups through the listening session for individual discernment, small group, and large group prayer times. The whole group can worship, eat, and fellowship together, of course.

If you are planning a retreat for a specific group, like a group of directors, or children's ministry workers, or small group leaders, or some such targeted group, encourage the leader (if that's you, then you do this) to expect a majority of your leaders to participate, for a couple of reasons. First, the prayer retreat experience is very powerful in bonding participants and in deepening their spiritual lives, two outcomes you want for all your leaders. Those who don't go will be missing a significant work in the life of both the leaders and the ministry. Second, events like a prayer retreat need to be seen as important enough to rise to the level of an expectation for leadership, not an add-on for leaders who have nothing else to do. While you will have some people with legitimate reasons for not being able to come, like childcare issues, illness, or conflicts that can't be avoided, your goal is that the majority of your leaders or team members make attending your prayer retreat a priority.

HOW DO I CONVINCE PEOPLE OF THE VALUE AND THE NEED FOR A PRAYER RETREAT?

Fruit of People at Prayer

One of the most powerful ways to show the value of a prayer retreat is to show people the fruitfulness of prayer. The best place to do that is to take people to God's Word. When people gather to pray, God hears and moves, and the Bible provides ample evidence of that. Consider the story of King Jehoshaphat in 2 Chronicles 20, who, when he was told a vast army was coming against him from Edom, proclaimed a fast for all Judah. Verse 4 tells us the people of Judah came together to seek help from the Lord (that may have actually been the largest group prayer retreat in history). The King's famous prayer has surely been echoed by thousands over the centuries, *"Lord, we don't know what to do, but our eyes are on you."*[40] As people from all over the nation entered into intercession, God spoke plainly, giving them direction as to next steps, resulting in a glorious deliverance as they obediently carried out the Lord's directives.

Move ahead a few thousand years, to the time of Jesus' ministry. After His resurrection, just before He

---

[40] 2 Chronicles 20:12 (NKJV).

rose into the clouds beyond sight, He instructed His disciples to go to Jerusalem and wait until they had received power from on high. So to Jerusalem they went, where over one hundred people gathered *to pray* as they obediently awaited the promised Holy Spirit: *"They all joined together constantly in prayer…"*[41]

Later in Acts we read the story of Peter's miraculous escape from prison. Is it too much to believe that the believers' prayers at the home of Mary, the mother of John Mark, *"where many were gathered together praying"*[42] played a significant role in Peter's release? We're told their prayers were not the only ones being offered—Acts 12:5 (NKJV) says, *"Peter was therefore kept in prison, but constant prayer was offered to God for him by the church."* Just these three examples from Scripture show the incredible power and fruitfulness of group prayer.

What about other historical examples? Here are just two that illustrate the power of corporate prayer. First, in what is now known as the "Miracle of Dunkirk," during World War II the Allied forces saw a miracle as a result of King George VI calling the nation to prayer on Sunday, May 26, 1940. It was a desperate moment during the war. The British army was outmaneuvered and surrounded by Nazi forces, pushed up against the English Channel with no way of escape. Some 300,000 troops faced complete

---

[41] Acts 1:14a. (NIV).
[42] Acts 12:12 (NKJV).

Planning a Prayer Retreat

annihilation. In that critical moment, the King took to the airwaves to request the nation observe a National Day of Prayer. And what transpired as the nation prayed? Actually three miracles: Hitler overruled his generals and halted an advance that most believe would have been successful; a terrible storm broke over Flanders that grounded the Luftwaffe, and finally, such a calm came over the English Channel that a vast armada of every kind of water craft was able to slip across the Channel and deliver the soldiers to safety on the other side.[43]

Move across the pond to the East Coast of the United States, and fast forward fifty-plus years to the days just after September 11, 2001. Though prayers in advance didn't subvert a catastrophe, corporate prayer *was* the response to a national tragedy. Dan Barry penned an article for *The New York Times* two weeks later, where he shared an event at the National Cathedral a day before, when then-President Bush and every other living past President joined him, with hundreds of others, to pray and mourn the tragedy of 9/11, as he called on the nation to pray and reflect. And it wasn't just Americans who came together to pray. Across the world nations expressed their condolences in corporate moments of silence and prayer, mourning the violence, interceding for all those affected, helping

---

[43] This account comes from David E. Gardiner, "The Miracle of Dunkirk," January 30, 3025, *Christians Together*, https://www.christianstogether.net/Articles/200052/Christians_Together_in/Christian_Life/The_Miracle_of.aspx

carry the weight of the tragedy in words too deep to speak.[44]

What miracles does your church, or ministry, or organization need? What afflictions might be best borne in the company of others, praying, reflecting, beseeching God to move on your behalf? Could God be calling you to call your group to prayer? Don't be shy about your invitation—this is the most powerful and important work you and your team will do. Believe that much will flow from your collective time of prayer, as it has in Scripture and throughout history. God will direct your actions, and your obedience will enable you to see the full fruit of the experience materialize.

It is vital to invest time in prayer before springing into motion, guided only by our human wisdom and ingenuity. Too often in the church, we move to action without ever taking the time to press in to God in rigorous corporate prayer. That reality is to our loss, for sure. You can be the one to establish a new cultural ethos in your organization, one in which we pray *first*, and then act. It's a model we all would do well to emulate. Once people are reminded of the fruitfulness of prayer as seen in the Bible and recent history, they will be more likely to be motivated to want to come.

---

[44] Dan Barry, "After the Attacks: The Vigils; Surrounded by Grief, People Around the World Pause and Turn to Prayer," Sept. 15, 2001, *The New York Times*, https://www.nytimes.com/2001/09/15/us/after-attacks-vigils-surrounded-grief-people-around-world-pause-turn-prayer.html.

Need

While your situation may not be as dire or at such a critical time in history as the two examples just shared, *something* is motivating you to consider planning a prayer retreat. One of the most compelling reasons people will join you on this retreat is if they understand the need to get away—even just overnight. You need to have clarity as to whether God is telling you to put a retreat together, or you just think it's a good idea in your natural awareness of circumstances. And, by the way, that's a justifiable reason to plan and lead a prayer retreat—I think it's *always* a good idea—so don't feel pressure to claim it's a Holy Spirit mandate if it isn't. If there are compelling needs that you and your group/ministry are facing, calling people to join you to intercede is reasonable, and will motivate those who are able to join you. You may also be motivated by other needs than those of your ministry, but perhaps the only reason you can articulate for extending a call to prayer is that you simply believe God has spoken. You may be wondering

> "Discernment does not mean knowing the difference between what is right and what is wrong. Discernment means knowing the difference between what is right, and what is almost right."
> —Charles Spurgeon

how you know if you are being led by the Holy Spirit or if it's just your own thoughts, idea, or will. Without writing a treatise, I would suggest a simple process of discernment. Did the idea seem to come out of the blue? Is it biblical? Does it stay with you over a period of time, coming back repeatedly accompanied by a sense of compunction—that compelling gut feeling that demands a response? I can sense when the Lord is moving because I get thoughts that I can't shake. They don't come with fear or apprehension, but they have a stickiness about them that compels me to act.

When I am moved with an idea for action I will put it before the Lord in prayer and ask Him to confirm that it comes from Him. Sometimes that means I take it to someone I trust and ask them what they think or to pray with me about it. Sometimes I run it by a spiritual authority. If I have done due diligence to weigh the prompting, then at the end of the day, I trust that I am hearing the Lord speak. You will move people if you suggest you have a holy mandate, so be sure to use this simple discernment method, or something like it, if you are going to lead with that!

You may also hear the Holy Spirit asking you to lead a retreat to intercede for needs *outside* your organization—for revival, for the lost, for the disenfranchised, for any cause that God attached to you for which you feel burdened to engage in extended prayer with others. The point is that, whether a mandate from God or a logical natural circumstance that calls for prayer, if people can see the need for the call, whether from God or from your concern, they will feel motivated to join you.

Personal Growth Opportunity

Another reason that can motivate invitees is recognizing the personal spiritual growth that will take place simply by their engagement in a prayer retreat. I can say from experience that the vast majority of people you will invite have never attended a *prayer* retreat. Yes, many people have gone on retreats, and yes, people have prayed while on those retreats, but very few people have gone on an overnight experience for the main purpose of praying. As you will see from the schedule, people will worship, people will eat, people will sleep, but the bulk of the time will be in prayer. This unique experience will stretch, enrich, challenge, and excite those who go.

For some, the thought of praying for extended periods of time will be daunting. As I mentioned, at one retreat I led, one of the long-time leaders pulled me aside and asked, "We aren't really going to pray this entire time, are we? Couldn't we just spend time relaxing and catching up with one another?" When I gently responded, "Well, actually, we really *are* going to pray for the majority of our time together," the look of incredulity on his face both amused me and made me nervous. If he didn't fully engage, I knew it could have quite a negative impact on the group. But, of course, God intervened. Consider how many of us have engaged in conversation with a friend that only ends when one says, "My goodness! Look at the time! We've been talking for hours!" Do we not believe God wants (and deserves) that same level of connection? He made "time," and He made "talk." As with our human relationships, God is honored when we give to Him what He has freely given to us—these gifts of time and attention. On this retreat, in short order my skeptical friend came to understand this truth. After two prayer gatherings during the first night, during the next morning's first prayer session my friend was reduced to tears—not just a few weepy drops, but the snot-inducing, catch your breath kind of crying that moved the rest of us to tears as well. I give my friend props for even coming given his misgivings, and you may also find people reluctant to attend. You can reduce the fear of the unknown by encouraging them with the assurance there will be good food, time to sleep and fellowship, structured times of prayer and worship, and even times for personal ministry, but emphasize that it will be a time of great personal growth and spiritual depositing by the Holy Spirit, as a result of the amount of time you will pray.

Who goes on a prayer retreat? People who see the value from the biblical and historical evidence, those with felt needs, those who desire personal growth. As you can see, that really means anyone and everyone. Be confident as you sense the stirrings of the Spirit to promote the notion of a group prayer retreat. There are compelling motivations from the Bible, human history, and the testimonies of God's miraculous moving as His people gather to pray.

CHAPTER FOUR

WHAT EXACTLY IS A PRAYER RETREAT?

> *"True prayer is neither a mere mental exercise nor a vocal performance. It is far deeper than that—it is spiritual transaction with the Creator of Heaven and Earth."*
> —Charles Spurgeon

This is where it starts to get fun, because I get to share a blueprint with you for group prayer retreats that is unique to anything I had ever experienced prior to leading my first one. I get excited about sharing it because it was a Holy Spirit download. Now, please don't hear me saying that no one else in the world has ever led or gone on group prayer retreats that contained similar elements. I am sure that is *not* true. What I am saying is that I had no external sources available to know what constituted a group prayer retreat. I really wanted to teach my students how to seek God in this way, to facilitate their experiencing extended time in God's presence in prayer, so I sought God for insight into what a prayer retreat could look like. In response to my prayers, He gave me a guide to follow that has proved to be effective over the decades with vastly different groups. While not every prayer retreat has been a "ten," as I shared earlier, this general structure for a group prayer experience has proved reliable and effective. Before I lay out this structure, let me describe the key components.

Prayer

This is a giant "duh," I know, but you might be surprised how many people go on a prayer retreat and don't expect to do that much praying. I am not sure why the disconnect exists, but I can tell you it does. Let's establish at the outset that prayer is the core of a group prayer retreat. Types of prayer include: individual time to seek the Lord for specific prayer direction for the retreat; small group prayer consisting of three or four people, depending on the size of your attendance; large group prayer; and soaking prayer for individual needs. For clarity, "soaking prayer" means an extended time of prayer for one individual. It can include prophetic praying; praying scriptures over the person; or prayers for healing or deliverance. It often addresses a need they have shared, although that is not necessary.

Worship

Worship is a critical component of prayer retreats for many reasons. While not all praise and worship songs can be classified as "prayer," or "communicating with God," many songs are forms of prayer. The act of corporate worship prepares the individual, but it also establishes the Holy Spirit's presence over the group, providing a collective sense of unity in the Lord, of shared purpose and identity for the duration of the retreat. Worship turns our attention away from the distractions of the world—the kids at home, the demands of work, the daily cares and concerns. Worship tills the soil of our hearts and minds, turning up the fallow ground of distance between us and the Lord. Worship provides space for "*Deep calling to deep*"[45] as we enter into the Holy of Holies to commune with God. For all of these reasons, worship should be a part of your prayer retreat.

The quality of the worship matters as much as its inclusion in the schedule. If you are blessed to have talented singers and musicians in your church, then, Glory! Get those folks to your retreat, whatever it takes. If you don't have attendees who can provide meaningful worship sessions, then there are other options. You can invite an outside person to provide the worship for the event. For one event, I invited my daughter, a seasoned worship leader, and she in turn brought a young woman with her to provide backup

---

[45] See Psalm 42:7

vocals. The worship was beautiful, and it set the tone well for prayer. At another retreat there was no one who could lead worship, so we used selected online videos and put together a montage of worship songs to facilitate group worship. The words were on a TV screen, the quality of music was professional, and the technology was not difficult. These are just a few examples of how to include worship during your prayer retreat.

The style of worship doesn't matter. Groups can enter deeply into worship through almost any modality: hymns, Gregorian chants, old-time choruses, or more modern five-part story songs, as long as the style is one with which the majority of your group will be familiar. While style is not a major factor, quality is. Forgive me if this is offensive, but having been a part of worship ministries for over two decades, I really believe that "bad" worship—lacking in talent or quality, even when led by sincere followers of Jesus—is worse than no worship at all.

Additionally, high quality worship that lacks the Holy Spirit's anointing, or is performance-driven, is also something to avoid. Look for talented, mature, anointed worshipers either within your church ranks or outside your local body who can lead several sessions of worship, or tap someone to put together a playlist if you have no one who can do it "live." Whether live or through media, be sure to have words available either on handouts or displayed through technology. In summary, while it does add an extra layer of complexity to the planning and implementing, do include worship. It really will make a difference to your times of prayer.

Meals

Praying can be exhausting—especially praying for prolonged periods of time. While I have had people occasionally suggest that the prayer retreat be a time of fasting, I have chosen not to attempt that model yet (and maybe not ever). Why? Because going on a prayer retreat can be intimidating on its own; not eating for the entire experience seems to be an unnecessary hardship, at least for initial experiences. If groups become "regulars" at prayer retreats, they may be ready for the deeper plunge into praying and fasting, but my recommendation is, especially if this is a first time for most attendees, that you provide ample food, beverages, and snacks. The one retreat I feel was the least successful was that way because I had not brought enough snacks and beverages. The meals were ample, but the retreat was for college students, and they could not go between meals without having something to eat. I had to shoo people out of the kitchen several times; there wasn't fast food nearby, most individuals didn't drive themselves, and these were days before Uber EATS®. People were hungry for the last half of the retreat. Please learn from my experience! Provide enough food and snacks to fuel people's bodies, and the return on investment will be worth it.

The ways to attend to meals, snacks, and beverages vary, depending on how much help you

Planning a Prayer Retreat

have, as well as how many people attend your retreat. If you are handling this responsibility, write out the number of meals you need to provide, what you want to serve, and an accompanying grocery list. You can either include snacks on your list or ask attendees to bring their favorite snacks to share. Follow the same process for beverages. Some venues require you to use their meal services—the upside is you have this detail taken care of; the downside is it typically costs more money.

You may be blessed with someone who can take on this responsibility for you. This person may want to attend prayer sessions as they are able, or they may wish to be the designated cook/kitchen boss and focus their time and energy on filling that role. Additionally, they may want or need to bring support help with them. Use your judgment on what is necessary, given the number of meals and number of attendees. You can also assign different small groups to help out with a meal set up and clean up. If you do have someone other than yourself who will oversee the meals/snacks/beverages, get them on board several weeks before the retreat, then meet with them several days before the retreat to finalize details and be sure everything is covered.

Given the proliferation of allergies and other health restrictions, you may want to gather attendees' dietary information on your registration forms. If your group is so small that you don't need a formal registration process, still take the time to check in with every registered attendee to make sure the planned menu includes food everyone can eat.

Fellowship

A last and vital component to the prayer retreat is time for fellowship, but it may look different than anticipated by some people who have gone on other retreats. There won't be chunks of free time to hang out or planned recreational activities in this model. Mainly, fellowship occurs during meals and in the evenings after the last prayer and debrief session of the day happens. By the end of the evening, most people are tired and just want to go to sleep, but sometimes, especially with younger people, there is still energy for talking over a cup of hot chocolate or a soda. During these focused prayer retreats, the facilities may offer a hot tub, sauna, or even a pool, which provide wonderful fellowship places for your group.

Discourage activities like watching movies, playing video games, or other forms of secular entertainment that can move the atmosphere away from devotional or sacred space. This might sound weird—but trust me, once you've "soaked" various rooms with hours of prayer, watching a movie or playing video games is counterproductive to maintaining a holy atmosphere. Keep it low key. Encourage beautiful and even hard conversations. Carry one another's burdens. Let the fellowship add to the presence of God by making sure He is glorified in whatever activities you provide or suggest for your attendees.

Planning a Prayer Retreat

You now have an overview of the basic components that make up a Group Prayer Retreat. Let's move on to some of the other details as we explore advice for the "where" and "when" of your retreat.

CHAPTER FIVE

WHERE AND WHEN SHOULD GROUP PRAYER RETREATS OCCUR?

"...sometimes the most spiritual advice we can give to someone is, 'Go get a snack.'"

Sometimes the most spiritual advice does not seem "spiritual" at all, but those of us who have walked this Christian path for more than a few years recognize that sometimes the most spiritual advice we can give to someone is, "Go get a snack." A second deeply spiritual piece of advice is, "Go take a nap." Upon first glance, those golden gems seem rather secular, but if you are attuned to our holistic nature as human beings, they make sense. Caring for our minds, souls, and bodies is an act of stewardship. Counseling ourselves or others in such practical ways is, therefore, deeply spiritual. The same principle applies to planning a Group Prayer Retreat. While it is fun and fundamental to strategically think through the spiritual components of these retreats, it is significant to mind the practical elements as well. They really can make or break the experience, and even influence whether or not people will willingly attend. We talked about the importance of food in the last chapter, which is a great example of this principle. Likewise, details such as time and place are equally important. If the place and time are not convenient, or at least doable in people's minds, they won't go, or if they "have" to go, they will arrive with such negative attitudes that it will impact the success of the event for everyone. We do well as leaders to prayerfully and carefully attend to such earthly details as location and date. This may seem like an obvious point, but perhaps what should go without saying is not always apparent. So, let me say it anyway! Here are some basic guidelines to keep in mind as you consider where and when to hold your event.

WHERE DOES ONE HOLD A PRAYER RETREAT?

My advice on where to hold a retreat can be summed up in six words: "Get away. But not too far!" While it would be wonderful if Christians valued praying together so much that they would be willing to be inconvenienced or expend extra effort to facilitate attendance, this is many times not the case. Until prayer retreats become a known and appreciated commodity in your organizational culture, their value-add is not readily apparent. If going on a prayer retreat requires a lot more work, or in any way is too great a "cost" (beyond the actual financial burden), people will not want to go. Especially for retreats that are just overnighters, you want attendees to be able to get there relatively soon after ending a work day, or picking up kids after school, or handing those kids to a spouse or grandparent. If the retreat is more than two hours away, this requires more planning and effort; it can limit the number of people who can get away.

While it may seem counterintuitive, the longer the retreat, the further people are willing to travel. For example, one three-day retreat (Friday through Sunday) I initiated was held at a location that required almost everyone to fly to the site, which everyone was willing to do. Based on the timeframe of your retreat, determine whether it should be within two hours by plane or by car. But you *will* want to get away. Do not hold the prayer retreat at your church or within ten or fifteen minutes of most people's homes. When the retreat location is in close proximity, some people will opt to go home to sleep, or just come for part of it, which can diminish the experience for them, as well as for the whole group. Also, if your location is too close to home, it seems harder for people to psychologically disconnect from their daily responsibilities, because they are still close enough to intervene, should they be needed. When you cross the thirty-minute barrier, it feels just far enough that you aren't as tempted to rush home or to work to "fix stuff." So, the first rule of thumb for your typical overnight prayer retreat is to look for something thirty to sixty minutes away. Next, find a place that has a kitchen where you can fix meals in-house, as in most cases, this will significantly help reduce costs, even if you pay someone to come fix the meals for your group. Besides allowing your group to prepare their own meals, it provides space to prepare snacks, store groceries and beverages, and do clean up throughout your event.

It is also important to find a location that has several separate places where small groups can gather for prayer. This is really important because the model that I have found to be successful is built around multiple small-group prayer sessions where each group of three to four people has a separate space to pray, free of the distraction of other groups within earshot. Additionally, there should be a large-group gathering space where all attendees can gather with room for seating as well as space to set up for worship (some worship instruments like keyboards take up significant square footage). This room should also be large enough to accommodate a white board or easels with large pads of paper. These are really the only "must haves" in terms of location specifications, but they do matter. It is my experience that most people are content to share sleeping quarters with others, especially if it is only for one night, and even for multi-night events, I have found most people are willing to share rooms and bathrooms as long as they can bring their own pillows (I'm only mostly kidding there!).

WHEN IS THE RIGHT TIME TO HOLD A PRAYER RETREAT?

There is no right time for a prayer retreat; it depends on your group and the purpose of the retreat. If there are crises that are best addressed through intense, prolonged prayer, then the group will likely be willing to prioritize a prayer retreat no matter what time of year or days of the week. If the prayer retreat is part of the regular rhythm of your ministry, then where it fits into the calendar is more discretionary. Looking at the comprehensive event schedule for the year and selecting a time that does not compete with preparation or implementation of other major events is optimal.

Consider holidays, vacation months, and travel-heavy dates and work around them. Avoiding the weeks or even months close to Christmas also takes holiday spending into consideration. Depending on the socioeconomic status of your group, if each attendee will be paying to take part, it can be wise to plan your retreat some months away from Christmas, as typically expendable income is diverted to holiday expenses immediately

> If there are crises that are best addressed through intense, prolonged prayer, then the group will likely be willing to prioritize a prayer retreat no matter what time of year or days of the week.

before and after December.

VENUE AVAILABILITY AND SCHEDULING YOUR RETREAT

Another important factor to consider when selecting dates for your retreat is the availability of venues. For retreat centers and camps, there can be high-demand seasons or even weekends such as Mother's Day or other holiday weekends when costs are higher due to demand. It is helpful to do your homework related to costs as you determine when to hold your prayer retreat by calling several places to check availability as well as price. Once you have a couple of options for place and dates, check with your group to get an initial idea of who will be able to attend. Doing this preliminary confirmation will save you the disappointment of planning the prayer retreat, only to discover that half of your hoped-for attendees already had obligations on those dates.

Do keep in mind, as well, that it is difficult to find a time that works for everyone if the retreat is being held for volunteers and/or members of a team or community where attendance is voluntary. When a paid staff retreat is organized, full attendance is more probable, yet conflicts or conditions can still arise, making participation uncertain. Take heart, however. God knows who needs to and should be there. As the organizer, if you walk through the steps to make attendance as low-threshold as possible, people will come. Ultimately, if a prayer retreat is supposed to

Deborah J. A. Miller, ED. D, D. MIN.

happen, with attention to best practices in the planning, your event will move forward and be a huge blessing to those who are able to go.

CHAPTER SIX

THE PRAYER RETREAT FLOW

> "The life of the prayer meeting...is dependent upon the release of the spirit of prayer...The key to this abandonment to the Spirit is sensitivity. Such sensitivity is cultivated by time spent meditating in God's Word, in worship, and in private prayer—in essence, by exposure to the presence of God."
> —Curran, *The Praying Church*, 56.

This is the most important chapter in this Guidebook. I am fairly certain that most of the other information—aside from my personal story and the Scripture review—falls into the category of common sense, though I believe each chapter provides a good reminder of details that should not be forgotten, as well as insights gained from experience. However, this chapter outlines the format I have used successfully over many years to lead group prayer retreats—one of the few models available to provide guidance for such an event. I have done several internet searches to find a book or an article or *some* source that outlines how to run a group prayer retreat. I couldn't find one twenty years ago, and, after a very recent search, can attest that if there is one out there, it isn't popping up on any web search that I've done. Not only is this one of the rare models you will find, but it is a tried and true one; this structure seems to contribute powerfully to the success of a prayer retreat. While this format is easily modified or adaptable, following the basic guidelines will assure that once you and your group arrive and begin to move through the agenda, God will meet you there to move in your midst. As mentioned previously, while planning my first-ever retreat, this design came to me as a Holy Spirit download. It's a blueprint that has worked for me with any group, of any age, for any purpose. And I'm very excited to share it with you!

Now that the details are in place…

You've got your list of attendees, made arrangements for meals, gathered your supplies, got your worship planned—it's time to think about the agenda. Of course, as you read the schedule with time frames, please recognize that while you direct your group's event you can modify these windows as the Spirit leads you. Through experience, I have learned the importance of including each element, but we should always leave room for the Holy Spirit to move uniquely in, through, and around the schedule. As you gain practice in facilitating group prayer retreats, you will become sensitized to the Spirit's voice directing the flow of the event. I do know, in general, that each retreat I have led has contained these elements in this order, and it has been a "Spirit formula" that seems to be conducive to believers having a deep and meaningful experience with God. So, at least for your first prayer retreat, I would encourage you to follow the format fairly closely, unless you hear a very direct word from the Lord to go in a different direction. I share this because there will be those in attendance who are ready to make many "suggestions" for what you ought to do, both before and during the retreat. Of course, a humble posture of receptivity is the appropriate response, but unless you really sense the Holy Spirit is speaking through them, affirm you are listening, but tell them you are committed to the format you've planned and hope they will support you in implementing it. Remind them that there will be time to debrief the event afterwards, and you will welcome their feedback. Feel confident to stand behind the plan, especially if you have prayed into it and trust that God has given you a blueprint to guide you. So here's that blueprint.

Deborah J. A. Miller, ED. D, D. MIN.

DAY ONE

As people arrive, let them find their sleeping quarters (either assign them or let them select from what's available) and then have everyone gather together in a central location large enough for comfortable seating. Share with them the format for the retreat, including the plan for meals and free time to assure them you have made plans for those all-important aspects of the retreat. And this is no joke; while these are not directly related to prayer, hearing you explain that you have accommodated for breaks, meals, and rest will help people focus on the times of prayer and worship without worrying about when they will get to eat, sleep, and use the bathroom. When you have given the group a *brief* overview of the event from start to finish, go back to the beginning and describe the opening session that will take you until the first break (usually dinner, but your schedule may start earlier in the day). Introduce the worship team if they are guests, and have everyone prepare for worship. Worship together for twenty to thirty minutes. It is preferable either to use songs that are very familiar, or to provide words as

> "Prayer should rise more out of God's Word and concern for His kingdom than even out of our personal needs, trials, or desires."
> —Forsyth, *The Soul of Prayer*, 91.

Planning a Prayer Retreat

handouts or on a screen or smart TV. Remember, if you do not have talented musicians who can lead, use technology to provide this experience. End this time of worship by having you or another leader close in prayer.

After worship, thank the team, then explain in detail the next activity, which is a critical step to the prayer sessions that will follow. The group is going to enter a discernment session, during which each person will individually draw away for twenty-five to thirty minutes to hear from the Lord. This is a time for the group to discern the topics to be addressed in prayer during the retreat. The instructions should be as follows: "For the next twenty or so minutes, each of us will spend time on our own asking God what topics we should be praying about during this retreat." For an overnight experience, I generally ask people to come up with three items for which to pray: one item specific to the ministry/organization or church, one related to society at large—a local, national, or international issue that can be political, cultural, social, etc., and lastly, a personal item—anything that God lays on their heart. Note that "personal" means a general prayer topic of their choosing, not something personal like, "Pray for my Aunt Rose." It would be topics like the persecuted church, or a missionary the church might sponsor, a humanitarian crisis or a world concern. This last item will fall into a category I label "Potpourri." If the retreat is a prayer retreat of a particular group, such as the women's or men's ministry, or outreach ministry, or whatever, you might ask attendees to think of a prayer request related to that specific ministry, then the church or organization of which the ministry is a part, and then one random prayer request for the potpourri column. If your organization is in crisis or the goal is to truly focus on prayer for that ministry, then you would limit the categories to just one; ask people to write down three specific issues that need to be covered in prayer with the singular focus on the ministry and its needs.

You can give this activity more time if your retreat is two overnights, as your attendees will need to generate more than three items for prayer; generally, for two or more nights, four to five topics of prayer per person are sufficient to create a focus for each of the sessions to follow. I also ask that if they have time they should ask God to provide a scripture to support the prayer request—either a promise or a command or admonition related to each topic they've written. I provide sticky notes for attendees to write on, but these are not absolutely necessary. If it is helpful, provide an example for each category, so they can be confident that they understand what they are being asked to do. Tell them how much time they will have, what you want them to do, and remind them that this is an individual activity. Encourage them to find a spot in your location that is semi-private so they will not be distracted or tempted to engage in conversation, then release them to this task. Check the time, and if you need to, write the time on a sticky note or your white board so you remember when to call them back together. While attendees are in this individual time seeking the Lord, prepare a white board or chart paper with the headings "Church/Ministry" (if you are leading a retreat for an organization, put the name of the organization or your department/division in this column), "Needs of the World," and "Potpourri." Depending on the focus of the retreat, your category titles will reflect whatever you assigned. When time is up, call people back to the central gathering place. If it seems necessary, encourage them to use the restroom or grab a snack or beverage, as the next session needs everyone present and engaged so everyone may get the most out of the rest of the retreat. At this point, you are moving into gathering their prayer topics and discerning how to group and order them to guide the prayer time over the rest of the retreat.

Let people know that the next step will take around forty-five minutes to an hour, and that the goal is to compile a list of prayer topics for your prayer sessions. In no particular order (unless it makes sense for you to go in a particular order) ask the participants to come up and take a couple of minutes to share with the group their three prayer topics and scriptures. As they share, have them place their sticky notes on the white board under the aligned heading. You or your leader will need to skillfully pace this activity, encouraging participants to volunteer to share as well as keep the sharing to the suggested window (occasionally folks will want to over-explain the rationale for their choices or preach a sermonette on the Bible verses they chose). If you don't use sticky notes for this exercise, you can have people remain seated and share their topics with the group while you or your scribe write the requests under each category on the white board. Either method works fine.

Now is a good time to suggest appointing a scribe for your prayer retreat—from this point on, it can be helpful to have a designated person other than yourself to record the work of the retreat. This person's assigned task will be to keep a written account of prayer topics, feedback, insights shared, moments of prayer that seemed most significant, and any other moments he or she feels the need to capture. While not absolutely essential, having a scribe will produce a narrative of the event that can prove useful for a variety of reasons.

Okay, so, back to the flow of the agenda. As people begin to share their prayer topics, you will see some duplication. This is a very good thing for a few reasons. First, as repetition of needs begins, it becomes apparent God is revealing a need that demands prayer attention. Additionally, people will be encouraged to see how the Holy Spirit has prompted multiple people to suggest prayer on the same topics. Finally, though perhaps counter intuitively, it is also good when people hear something very "out of the box" offered as a prayer topic (these usually land in the potpourri category, but not always) because it adds flavor to the prayer times and typically resonates with others as a true need when they hear it shared. As you progress through this part of the agenda, it is helpful to realize it

Planning a Prayer Retreat

is not possible to cover more than ten to twelve prayer topics in one overnight retreat and not more than fifteen in a two-night retreat, so depending on the size of your group, you will most likely have to begin to group sticky notes together that are similar in order to intercede for all of them. As you see themes repeated, move those sticky notes together in the same area of the white board to eventually become one prayer topic. Encourage the group to help you or the facilitator in this process to find connections and commonalities. Again, the goal is to develop ten to twelve prayer topics that will become the focus of each of your intercession times for the rest of the retreat. When you are finished with this process, people will be excited, but also will need a break, so give them a short one and tell them to come back ready to get started PRAYING!

During this break, either with a co-leader, the scribe, or on your own, prioritize the prayer topics by category and groupings. I prefer having someone assist me in this process; this would typically be the head of the department or ministry for which I'm doing the retreat, or the head pastor or someone else on staff. If that person is you, then find an Aaron or Hur that is willing to go with you on the retreat and be your arm upholder. It's always better to have another pair of ears and eyes! Once you've gotten your topics grouped and categorized, prioritize them by category. You can choose to pray through all of the groupings in one category first, and then move to the next category (remember, we've created categories of the church

/your ministry, the world, and potpourri, or your group, the church, the world, or whatever categories you have); or you can choose to rotate through the categories a couple of topics at a time, based on how you prioritized them. It doesn't seem to matter. Before attendees return from break, select the first four prayer topics.

PREPARING TO DEPLOY: A Timeframe and Guidance in Group Prayer

In this part of the chapter I am going to explicitly walk through giving directions to the group about how the prayer sessions will work. I have worked in education for four decades, and a basic principle I have found to be true regarding learning is the Feynman Technique. Richard Feynman was a 20th Century American theoretical physicist and Nobel laureate. He came up with a four-step process for learning that is profound for its wisdom and simplicity. It states that one of the key steps to measure whether or not you fully understand a concept is to explain it as if you were talking to a child. His belief was if you can't explain it to a child, you don't fully grasp the concept yourself. Based on that idea, I am testing my own grasp of the process of guiding people through a prayer retreat by sharing with you, my reader (yes, I know you are not children…just work with me!) I hope by giving these explicit directions here, the process will be clear to you. When people re-gather, give them these instructions: "For the next hour or so, we will cover two prayer topics, then take a break. We will divide you into groups of three or four (five would be max), give you one prayer topic, and then your group will have twenty minutes to pray on that topic. Please set a timer, and after twenty minutes come back to get the next prayer topic."

At this point, I almost always take time to explain a model of group prayer that is truly praying *"together"* in prayers of agreement and in the flow of the Holy Spirit. This model of prayer may be more associated with charismatic churches or more spontaneous forms of worship, but in truth, it simply represents praying together, rather than praying separately while being in proximity. In this form of intercessory group prayer, one person begins praying on the assigned topic as they are led by the Holy Spirit. He or she will have a particular focus. When they have prayed what is on their mind, they should stop and let someone else pick up that thread and add to it. If no one else picks that thread up, then either they or someone else in their group can offer up prayer on the assigned topic from a different focus. Let me give you an example for clarity. If the group is assigned the topic of praying for singles in the church, one person may start by praying for single moms and their financial needs. After they finish their prayers for single moms, they should

> Being in sync with the Holy Spirit and with each other in intercessory prayer means listening to each other and the Holy Spirit.

pause and allow the Spirit to prompt someone else in their group to pray for single moms. A different person may pray for single moms and their relationship with their children. When they are finished praying from that perspective, they pause to see if anyone has anything else they want to pray for single moms. After a few seconds, if no one else starts praying for single moms, anyone should feel free to start praying for a different set of singles—like widows, those who are separated, or those who have never been married and are looking for spouses. The point is one person doesn't start praying and decide to cover single moms (or dads), the widowed, the newly divorced, the young adult seeking a mate…and just pray for ten minutes without taking a breath. And then, upon finishing, the next person picks up the prayer baton and simply prays the same list all over again. In that model, it seems people are simply waiting their turn to pray their list, rather than truly entering into prayers of agreement as others are praying.

Being in sync with the Holy Spirit and with each other in intercessory prayer means *listening* to each other and to the Holy Spirit to "pray through" a topic together, in agreement, in a "popcorn style" as the Spirit leads. Praying popcorn style allows everyone to be engaged in praying out loud like a conversation with each other and the Lord, as our prayers stir each other to make intercession aloud and agree with each other. Most people appreciate the reminder and recognize that this makes prayer far more dynamic and engaging.

Planning a Prayer Retreat

With that, dismiss them. Expect it will take them time this first go-around to find that just-right place for their group, and settle into prayer. You and your support friend can circulate throughout the facility to assist in settling teams and encourage them to pray. Especially during this first round, people's prayer motors are not warmed up; inevitably it takes a little bit of verbal encouragement for people to start praying. At the end of the twenty minutes (don't start the "clock" right away for this first session, as it takes a few minutes for groups to settle in the first time), give an "all call," gather everyone back together, and give them their next topic. Tell them that after this topic you will be taking a dinner break (or just a break, depending on when you started). Send them out for round two, with a time to return in twenty minutes. They will be starting to feel the energy of prayer. At the end of twenty-ish minutes, call them back together.

While the group is praying, make sure you have your next two topics, so you are ready for the next hour of prayer. At twenty minutes, call them back together, and take ten minutes to debrief the two prayer sessions. Ask questions like, "Was it hard to get into? What insights is God giving you? How did you feel led to pray on those topics?" Don't be too exhaustive with this, as the debrief is designed to gather initial feelings/responses, not to rehash the entirety of the experience. If it is dinner time, go to the meal. If it isn't, take a quick break to get snacks and drinks, use the restroom, or take a quick walk, then come back to two more prayer topics if you can get these in before dinner.

As the facilitator, you will need to determine with the group leader how many prayer sessions will fit in before the dinner hour and after. Some groups are able to pray for three or four sessions the first day they arrive because they are able to start working through the agenda in the early afternoon, enabling them to cover eight topics in just the first day. However, you don't want to push so hard that praying feels like a grind. If the retreat starts on a typical work day, the earliest most retreats can get started is around 5:00pm. Whenever you are able to start, as you work through the prayer sessions, watch for people's energy and focus and adjust your schedule accordingly.

After the dinner break, the group will have another opportunity to worship. This worship set should be two to three songs, ten to fifteen minutes in length. While it may seem unnecessary, taking time to worship is very restorative, and tends to recharge people for the next prayer sessions. At the end of this time, you can reset the groups if it seems necessary (sometimes it's best to mix them up; other times the groups have gelled, have nice chemistry and don't want to change). Give them their next assignment and send them out for twenty-five minutes. After twenty-five minutes, re-gather them, give them their next topic, and redeploy them. By now, your group has spent time in individual prayer, worshipped together, discerned prayer direction together, and prayed through at least four prayer topics.

> "And he told them a parable to the effect that they ought always to pray and not lose heart." Luke 18:1

After this last time of prayer, do another debriefing. Let the feel of the room determine how much formal debriefing is needed. When people have shared with the large group what they've experienced so far, "call it a night" and release people to talk, sleep, take advantage of any amenities provided by the site such as a hot tub or basketball court, or unwind in whatever way they need. Do encourage them to avoid working, engaging with social media, or finding other common distractions. Typically, people from teens to seniors are very tired after praying, but also very wired. I have taken teens who do not want to stop praying—in one case we kept going through the prayer topics until midnight and I somewhat reluctantly forced a stop for the evening! Remind the group when breakfast will be served. Take a break yourself after making sure worship and breakfast plans are ready for the morning.

DAY TWO

You can set the start of the day for whatever time you want. Usually, this is affected most by what time you are ending the prayer retreat and how many prayer sessions you want to hold before the end of your time together. Typically, breakfast should be somewhere in the 7:30am to 8:00am time frame. This is typically a bit of a "sleep in" for most people who have to get children ready for school and/or get to work. Half an hour is sufficient for breakfast, unless you are on more than an overnighter, in which case your time frame can be more leisurely. Ask people to convene in the large group gathering space at a prescribed time after breakfast (you can make breakfast optional, if you like). Let's say you set breakfast in the 8:00 to 8:30 window. Ask attendees to gather in the large-group gathering space for worship when breakfast ends. Your worship team should be ready to go (or you should have the worship songs/set pulled up and ready to play) for the sake of time. Spend twenty to thirty minutes in worship, then close the worship time with prayer.

Next, instruct those gathered that the first prayer session of the day is for them to personally connect in a time of "listening" to the Lord for their own lives. While this may seem odd to do as a part of a "group" prayer retreat, it serves a couple of important purposes: First, it encourages those who may not have a regular time of devotions in their personal lives to experience what a designated time alone with the Lord feels like. Second, it gives each one a reprieve from the voices of others so they can simply listen to the voice of the Lord attending to their souls—comforting, challenging, encouraging, directing. If you are leading a group that contains younger-in-the-Lord Christians, remind them as you send them out that each one of them has the capacity to hear from God—that "His sheep know His voice."[46] Encourage them to wait in a listening posture and expect God to speak. Invite them to use all their senses to engage with the Lord's presence and to be observant as to how the Lord might speak through nature, through common items that can become symbols. Encourage journaling so they can capture in writing what they hear the Lord speaking. Make these comments brief—not a sermon—so that people can be released to spend time with the Lord. With a quick reminder to find a quiet, solitary space, let them know what time you would like them to re-gather. Thirty minutes for this time of personal prayer should suffice.

When everyone gathers after personal prayer, direct attention to the white board where you are moving through the prayer categories together. By now, you probably have half your topics covered, so you should have five or six topics left. Assign the first and send everyone out to pray. You may want to reassign groups; if so, do it without a lot of discussion for time's sake and so that feelings don't get involved. While it might be surprising, even on a prayer retreat of mature believers you may have people who struggle with feeling rejected as well as those who can get "cliquish." Your swift reassignments help avoid any uncomfortable moments of, "Hey, be with me!" or of someone being left out if the participants regroup themselves. Follow the same format as the previous

---

[46] John 10:27.

day, calling the groups back together after each round of prayer, giving them their next assignment, and then redeploying them for prayer. Do this twice (cover two prayer topics), then provide a ten-to-fifteen-minute break to attend to personal needs and just reset brains. A note on the twenty-minute prayer windows: As you facilitate, your goal is to provide the right pacing to cover two prayer topics an hour. Moving in and out of prayer takes a few minutes, typically three to five minutes on either side of prayer. I keep to the rhythm and pace fairly consistently; it provides structure for attendees, keeps the momentum going, and allows for the prayer topics generated by the group to be covered over the course of the retreat. During this time, the facilitator is either joining a group to pray, checking the progress through the agenda and re-organizing topics, making sure meals/beverages/snacks are refreshed or on schedule, or even sometimes handling difficulties with facilities or counseling individuals in crisis.

By now, it will be around 10:30am. You will be watching the clock closely depending on what time you committed to ending your retreat. I highly recommend ending on time, or as close as possible, even if it means combining topics for the last group prayer sessions or assigning groups different topics. Realistically, if the retreat is set to end at noon, either with lunch and then departure, or just before lunch so everyone heads out to a restaurant or is on their own to grab lunch on the way home (alternatively, you can also provide sack or box lunches if you like), you have time for one more set of prayer topics and a short debriefing session. Based on the time, you can use this last block in a number of ways that have been effective for me in the past. You would choose which one based on your group, how important the last topics seem to be (it is hopeful you started with the most weighty so that your heavy topics are not left to cover), and exactly how much time you have left. Here are three ways I have used the closing session(s):

Option One: Finish your last round of two prayer topics, and debrief for fifteen to twenty minutes. It is really important to have some sort of group wrap-up, so don't just pray until the very last minute, grab your suitcases, and run out the door. The prayer times will still have been efficacious and the effects of prayer powerful, but taking time at the end to come together, celebrate the good work the Lord did, recognize the camaraderie of extended praying that knits hearts together in one accord, and thank the worship team and the meal providers and whoever else contributed to the success of the event—all these seemingly minor items are actually very important. Calling everyone back together for even a short debrief also allows you or a designee to speak a benediction over the group and let them know what sort of follow-up there will be after your time together.

Option Two: Take whatever topics you have left to pray over and divide them among the different groups, giving all of the groups thirty minutes to pray through their topic(s). Then re-gather everyone and take thirty to forty minutes to debrief. Take time to do the activities mentioned above: thank those who had special assignments such as worship or meals; celebrate the success of the retreat; recognize the work that God did during your time together; and suggest what kind of follow up attendees can expect once you return home.

Option Three: If you only have one or two topics left that perhaps have been really "prayed around" during other prayer sessions, you may choose to devote this final session to praying for individual needs. If you know ahead of time that your group would benefit from this sort of prayer session, then build it into your schedule from the beginning, and organize your prayer list of sticky note items into fewer prayer topics in your three categories so that your last prayer session can be designated as a time to pray for individual needs.

Depending on the size of your group, you can choose to welcome everyone to receive prayer. It is likely that you have experienced praying for people, so you probably don't need a lot of direction here, but it may help if I describe what I mean by that. Simply, the person requesting prayer shares briefly the issues for which they want prayer, and then others in the group typically put a hand on them or extend a hand toward them and pray for that need, asking the Holy Spirit to lead their prayers. The actual praying itself is not the challenge. The biggest challenge by far that I've faced is the tendency for everyone to want to pray for everyone, which cannot be done in an hour if you have more than seven to eight people in attendance. The solution is simple, but not easy: either don't pray for everyone, or limit the amount of time spent praying for each individual.

The problem may be solved for you because the number of people who want prayer may not be more than seven or eight. Does that surprise you? It might be tempting to assume that everyone will want prayer, but that would not be a correct assumption—not everyone will want to be in the prayer "hot seat," and that is okay. Don't force it. But, in most settings, everyone will want to receive prayer. If this is your situation, then a way to handle the time constraints is to either appoint two people or ask for two volunteers to pray for each person. Do this after you have selected the person for whom you will be praying. Each of these options has its advantages. If the group is familiar with one another, having people pray who know each other well leads to specific and direct prayers, as well as displays of love and affection since they are interceding for someone they know and love.

Alternatively, if you as the leader select people who may not know the individual as well, the outcome can be just as impacting. It can be very interesting how the Holy Spirit will direct someone to pray in ways that seem almost prophetic (from my background, we would affirm that the Lord still gives words of knowledge and people can move prophetically when they pray). Especially after everyone has been engaged in prayer for an extended time already, the sensitivity to the Holy Spirit and the ability to discern have been sharpened, such that this time of prayer for each other can be extremely powerful (whether you choose to let people volunteer to pray for each other, or you select people to pray). Once this time of praying for individuals is over, you will still want to do the debriefing portion as a way to put a bow on the event. Again, even if it means running over even fifteen minutes, it is worth it to be sure this culminating conversation happens.

And… That's a Wrap!

Well, it's over. With the last session debriefed, all that's left is making sure the facility is left in whatever condition is required, and that you've swept through the location for any left behind cords, food in the fridge, or supplies and equipment. Before you close the door behind you and head out, be sure to gather the sticky notes and/or take photos of the images on the white board. This will be important information for you to have when you return home.

You've come to the end of the prayer retreat. You will be tired, but extremely fulfilled. Your spirit and soul have been nourished over the past twenty-four or more hours, and though your mind and body are weary, your heart will be very full. Enjoy your sense of accomplishment. The Lord is pleased.

CHAPTER SEVEN

AFTER THE EVENT

> "There is a deep joy in praying together, an added vitality, a plus difficult to define. It is rather like the difference between eating your meal alone and sharing in a party feast. Eating together is not the same as eating in solitude; the something more is the company, the fellowship. So it is with prayer."
> —Stephen Winward, *Teach Yourself to Pray*. (London: Hodder, 1961) 8.

There will be some follow-up work for you to do after the event is over. If you were asked to lead this prayer retreat by another leader for their group or ministry, then your role post-event will be to suggest certain action items as a way for them to follow up. You can offer to help, but at this point you have done what you were asked to do—lead a prayer retreat—so your work is done. If you led this prayer retreat as a part of your role as a leader of a group or ministry, then this is your work to do. And it is important to do it so the impact of the prayer retreat can continue in the lives of those who attended, and so others in your church or ministry who were not at your event also are aware of its impact.

First, be prepared to provide a summary for church leaders and staff, providing specifics on your prayer sessions, sharing any prophetic words or images the group may have received, and recounting the ways you believe it impacted those who attended. Share with them the images you took of the prayer request topics, people engaging in prayer, worship, the facility, or any other photos that capture the heart of the event. If there were challenges, you can share them, but definitely focus on the positive. Give other leaders or team members a taste of what the experience was like. Consider the following information as you prepare your brief report:

POST-RETREAT REPORT TEMPLATE

- Group name (men's ministry leaders; small group leaders; high school student council, etc., board of directors)
- Dates of the event
- Location of the event
- Number of people who attended

- Very brief summary of the schedule (number of prayer sessions, total number of hours spent in prayer)
- Examples of prayer topics covered during the retreat
- Two brief stories of highlights, perhaps drawn from the debrief times or the feedback responses from those who attended
- Your one- to two-sentence summary of the impact of the retreat as it relates to the purpose for which it was held

Be sure to include photos (and be sure to include photos of people praying, not just eating, fellowshipping, or sitting in a hot tub.

Next, you will want to suggest or do two follow-up activities with those who attended. First, you should send either a handwritten or email thank you note (you know your community, so do whatever would convey the appropriate thanks in your context) to each of the attendees, with one caveat—if you had more than eight people attend, it is acceptable to forego a handwritten note and send a group email message to everyone who attended with a quick note of gratitude and a recap of the work the Lord did. Share a couple of personal highlights for you as the leader. Consider including some photos to stimulate their memory of the event. This thank-you should arrive in mailboxes or inboxes no more than two weeks after the event—or don't send it. Any longer than two weeks and it feels like an afterthought—not the message you want to communicate!

Following the thank you note, and perhaps even included with it, you should send a very brief survey in order to procure feedback. This survey does not need to be anything complicated or formal, though if you know your people and something more formal would resonate resulting in a better rate of return, then by all means go ahead and develop a formal survey. There are several reputable sites with nice survey tools that are free and collect and display the data in chart form for easy comprehension and presentation. But if your group is more informal and might even be put off by a formal survey, then a few simple questions in paper or email form should suffice. Sample questions could include:

- What was your favorite part of the retreat?
- What would you change about the experience?
- Were you surprised that you could engage in prayer for a prolonged period of time? If so, how do you feel now about your capacity for extended prayer?
- What was your biggest take-away from the experience?
- What else would you like us to know as we think ahead to future prayer retreats?

This information will prove valuable as you plan future retreats and for reporting the impact of the retreat to others. At this point, you may be thinking, "I am not even on staff, so I am not accountable to report on the retreat," or possibly, "I run my department autonomously, so I don't need to share what happened," but I would encourage a broader perspective on gathering feedback. Even if you are not accountable for reporting on the event, for the sake of continuous improvement, for celebrating the work of God in people's lives, and in the event you may need to publicize for future events, gathering feedback from attendees is invaluable. Take the time to write the feedback survey and send it out to attendees.

Next, for your personal benefit and the benefit of future retreats, to the file folder where you kept your registration lists and other documents related to logistics, food, etc., add a page of notes, as detailed as possible, of what went well and what didn't. Look at the retreat from every angle: Were the sleeping quarters adequate? How about areas for food preparation and eating? Could you have accommodated more people? If so, how many? Would it have served you better with fewer people? Jot down your thoughts. The right facility can contribute or detract significantly from the overall success of an event. Think about the food. Was the menu right for the event? Were the food choices conducive to the purpose of the event? That may seem like an odd consideration, but certain foods can put people into a food coma, effectively shutting down any prayer intensity there was before the meal. Also, some meals take longer to prepare and serve or are significantly more expensive. Reflect on that, and take notes accordingly. How about the beverages? One Keurig is not enough for a group of fifteen people, unless you plan into the schedule fifteen minutes for everyone to get a cup of coffee, which I would not recommend (someone pointed out this would take two hours for just fifteen people—and by then, the line would be queued up for a second cup!).

How was the worship? If it met or exceeded your expectations, describe *why*. Was it the particular leaders? Their song choices? Details like this matter, and the better notes you take after your return home, the better prepared you will be for the next retreat. As you take time to build up your repository of prayer retreat notes, you will be able to draw on past experiences to design future retreats specific to an audience, selecting the place, meals, worship, and the rhythm of prayer and breaks based on the group and purpose of the event. Here is a template you can use to prompt your thinking.

POST-RETREAT NOTES

Retreat Site:
Retreat Dates:
Ministry or Organization:

Area	Positives (What worked well, and why)	Negatives/Issues/Challenges
Lodging		
Food		
Worship		
Registration Process		
Transportation		
Agenda/Schedule		
Cost		
Other Items to Consider		

CHAPTER EIGHT

STUFF TO THINK ABOUT

> Moving through activities is a Goldilocks endeavor—there really is a too fast, too slow, and just right.

WATCHING THE CLOCK

It may have surprised or even annoyed you as you read through the agenda and saw how precisely I provided windows of time for the various elements in the schedule. You may have asked, "Does it really have to be that rigid? Can't you just press "play" and let the event go as the Spirit would lead?" I can only respond, "Maybe?" because I've never done that. And it goes back to that very first high school prayer retreat. As I was praying about how to structure the time so the students could stay engaged, focus on prayer, be reinvigorated through worship, and have skin in the prayer game by praying through topics that mattered to them, the Lord revealed a prayer retreat design that could accomplish those goals. I trusted His leading, and it worked (go figure ☺). From my decades of experience as a classroom teacher, I also am firmly convinced of the benefit of pacing. Moving through activities is a Goldilocks endeavor—there really is a too fast, too slow, and just right pace. Linger too long in an activity without taking a break, and energy and focus are lost. Move too quickly, and people feel rushed and stressed. Hit that sweet spot of just right, and the momentum is palpable. Of course, throughout the years, different retreats have had different rhythms. Sometimes they are longer by a day. That invites a slower pace, as well as an ability to linger longer in morning devotions, or worship. Debriefings can go longer; prayer for individuals can be less directed and more "go with the flow." But in general, overnight retreats are successful when the leader moves through each section of the agenda within the window of time I've suggested, give or take ten to fifteen minutes, without making major adjustments.

BEHIND SCHEDULE! WHAT TO DO?

People will watch the clock, so if you are behind schedule, let people know you are aware of that, and tell them what your plan is to get back on track—are you going to cut short a prayer session? Push back a meal? Have a shorter worship time? Cut something out completely? Eat while you are debriefing? I have found that if people trust that you are not going to run over by more than twenty or so minutes with the formal program, they understand and it doesn't negatively impact their overall perspective of the retreat. It is also wise to let people know how the timeline is unfolding with regard to the ending on the last day, so they can make informed decisions about their own schedules. If people need a hard stop because of other responsibilities, knowing you won't be finishing on time is very important to them. Really, whether or not people have other responsibilities awaiting, it is respectful to ask people for permission to run past the designated ending if there is a final session for which a majority of your attendees are willing to stay. Watching the clock and communicating that you may go long also gives an opportunity for you to graciously release those who can't stay beyond the closing time so they don't have to awkwardly slip out.

WHAT IS "DEBRIEFING"?

I mentioned debriefing with the group a couple of times during the retreat. It occurred to me that some of you readers may not have led a group debriefing before; very likely most readers have not led a *prayer retreat* debriefing. I offered some sample questions as I shared the schedule with you, but I want to share a rationale so you will be convinced of its importance. So here's a brief description of what I do and why I do it.

After a few rounds of prayer, typically before releasing people to free time/bedtime on the first day, and then at the end of the retreat, gather attendees into the central meeting space. Let them sit comfortably wherever they want and if you want to encourage them to grab something to drink or eat, do, especially if dinner won't be ready right away. Ask people how they are feeling in general. Ask them how hard or easy it was to get into the groove of praying together. Ask about how they sense the Holy Spirit speaking to them and if it seems to be getting easier with each prayer session. Ask if there have been any "aha" moments for anyone, anything they have learned about themselves related to prayer, or about praying with others, or about praying in general. Your scribe should record these comments; if you don't have a scribe, try to capture some of these remarks in your journal, so that you can remember them for reporting and for promoting prayer retreats in the future.

During these debriefings, not everyone has to talk. It is okay to limit the feedback to two to three people in order to stay within the window of time allotted. Again, it is okay to spill over a little, especially if you are waiting for dinner. If you have a really big group, this debriefing can be done in pairs or trios, so that everyone does get a chance to share what they are experiencing and how they are processing it. As you allow time and space for debriefing, it can really help people to clarify how they are feeling.

And just a heads up: you may have someone share that they are struggling. If that is the case, take a moment to pray for that person. If possible, since the debriefing is usually followed by a meal or free time, spend some time with that person one on one to provide an empathetic listening ear. If more than one person admits they are struggling, and it seems like their challenges are related to an issue that is within your power to change, consider making an adjustment to accommodate for it. An example might be if their group is praying someplace too close to another group, and they are feeling really distracted. Help problem solve a new location for one group. Or perhaps the venue is too cold. Resolve the problem by turning up the heat or finding blankets. As you can see, debriefing has a lot of benefits, so don't bypass these times if at all possible.

WHAT IF SOMEONE ISN'T ENGAGING?

There will be times (I've experienced these) when someone has come on the retreat because they have to—say, the head pastor decides the whole staff will go on a prayer retreat, or an entire ministry team from a particular division is scheduled for a prayer retreat, or those committed to going on a mission trip are asked to take a 24-hour prayer retreat before leaving on the mission trip. Each of these instances offers an opportunity for someone to arrive at the prayer retreat location less than thrilled to be there. It isn't that people are opposed to prayer, per se. But it is true that:

    a. many people have undeveloped prayer lives, and may actually have never prayed aloud with another human being;

b. people's personal lives may be in a place of struggle due to trials, hardships, or even unconfessed sin making the thought of praying for twenty-four hours very uncomfortable, or

c. there are people who just don't like to be forced to do anything, much less spend twenty-four hours praying.

Fortunately, there are ways to sway the Doubting Thomases and Thomasinas, thanks be to God. In my experience, most of the resistance is going to come at the beginning of your time together. These individuals may or may not engage in worship, and may struggle to come up with any legitimate prayer topics to share with the group. They may drag their heels into the first prayer session, and engage very little in the actual prayer time. But what also is typical is that by the second or maybe the third (if they are hardcore resistant) prayer session, the Holy Spirit will begin moving on them and they will begin to respond to His presence. Perhaps this is due to God's grace or simply due to the fact that where God is present, we are hard pressed to maintain our resistance. Either way, the unengaged don't stay that way the entire time, so don't get discouraged if you can sense that resistance.

There are practical ways to help move the disengaged to engage so the Holy Spirit's influence can take effect as soon as possible. First, be really strategic in grouping this person or these people with your most committed and enthusiastic prayers. Second, if you see this person holding others back from engaging in prayer during the first session, then join that group during the second session to help the group stop talking to each other and start talking to God. If that individual remains a distraction and a reluctant pray-er, you may need to ask the leader (or if that's you, then YOU) to talk to the person in private and ask them to try to make the most of the opportunity or at least not prevent others from being fully engaged. These strategies should work to help everyone remain focused.

> Sometimes if you see diminishing engagement, what you are sensing is simply weariness.

Sometimes if you see diminishing engagement, what you are observing is simply weariness. This can be attributed to many factors—once 9:00pm comes, some of the older participants may be approaching their normal bedtimes. On the other end of the life stage spectrum, parents of young children may be so relaxed being off "kid duty" for a night that they get sleepy! Just pay attention to the general energy of the group, and if you need to cut a prayer time short and give a longer break or encourage people to grab a snack or beverage, then do.

Deborah J. A. Miller, ED. D, D. MIN.

WHAT IF SOMEONE IS TOO DOMINATING?

At times you may have people attend who are very enthusiastic about praying, have some leadership aspirations, and would be very happy to take over if you are willing to let them. Rarely is the motive malicious or personal. About thirty years ago at a youth conference, I heard a speaker share a line that has stuck with me over the decades: "*A weakness is just a strength overplayed.*" I turned that phrase around in my mind, examining it from every angle. Was it logical? Was it biblical? Did it ring true in my experience? Check, check, and check. In the context of a group prayer retreat, those with legitimate leadership skills often just want to be helpful. When they perceive there is space for their leadership or they simply want to exercise their leadership gift whether there is space for it or not, they will try to move into that role because it feels good to them and they like exercising their gifts.

Discerning that their motive isn't evil, but rather comes from immaturity or unawareness, you are able to respond graciously. But *do* respond. If they are over sharing when they have the floor, gently bring the conversation to an end by repeating, "Thanks for sharing. Maybe we could hear more later…" or "It sounds like you have a lot of insight into that area, but for the sake of time, we are going to need to keep moving!" or Hey, we have a few others who need to share, and our time is running out, so we're going to need to move on. However you choose to address it, do it.

Sometimes, this person will not try to take over in a large group setting, but will dominate during the small group prayer sessions. There are two effective ways to deal with this:

1. Before the first prayer session, as you are giving instructions for praying together, remind everyone that corporate prayer is shared prayer: everyone should feel free to pray on any topic, but everyone should also be sure others have a chance to pray on any topic. Remind them that prayer should begin almost immediately once the group is settled in their prayer space, without a lot of sharing or discussion preceding the actual prayer time.

2. Walk around the prayer site quietly during the first one or two sessions to make sure people are able to get settled in, and that no one is trying to dominate. Obviously, you want to do this unobtrusively. You are not circulating through the venue to give further instruction or involve yourself directly with the prayer groups. You are simply checking to see if everyone has what they need and all are doing okay. If you have concerns about a particular individual, you can hang around observing to see if they are taking too dominant a position, and if they are, you can remind the group at the next gathering

to be sure everyone's voice is being heard during the sessions.

Finally, with that person who seems to want to provide leadership through over sharing, dominating prayer times, or being too directive throughout the event, humbly and respectfully address the behavior through group direction, or, if absolutely necessary, a one-on-one conversation where you encourage them to self-limit. It will be very rare that a situation devolves to the need for a personal conversation; you will need to discern whether or not someone is dominating to the detriment of their small group or the overall event. If and when you discern that this person's behavior is having a negative effect on the group, it is important that you have the necessary conversation to make them aware of the impact of their behavior.

If this is a group that knows each other well, this person's personality and tendencies are most likely well known to others and there is a level of tolerance that allows this person to conduct him or herself as usual, to no one's great harm. In the rare case someone is truly trying to publicly highjack the agenda in a highly disruptive way, as the leader you owe it to the group to gently but firmly keep the event flowing as you believe the Holy Spirit is directing you, or you and the leader you are supporting. A kind but consistent, understated but confident authority to lead will assure the group that you are capable of directing a successful corporate prayer experience. Even if it is your first time leading, trust that God has prepared you and be confident that, even with older, louder, or persistent voices urging you take the agenda in a different direction, you have heard from the Lord and be at peace staying on track with the agenda that is planned.

WHAT IF SOMEONE WANTS THE FOCUS ON THEMSELVES AND THEIR PERSONAL NEEDS?

In general, people attend corporate or group prayer retreats as a part of a group or a team that is having a prayer retreat for a specific purpose. It might be to lay a foundation of prayer before setting the goals for the year; it might be because there is ambiguity or uncertainty around certain decisions; it may be there is a full-blown crisis that needs prolonged intercession. The point is that the vast majority of group prayer retreats have an established shared or common purpose, rather than simply being a, "Hey, let's all go away together and just pray for ourselves and each other on whatever random issues come up." Because those attending recognize the shared or common focus, most attendees will be very glad to spend the vast majority of the time praying for the needs of the church, the ministry, and the world, with little focus on themselves and their personal needs. As mentioned, a closing time of prayer for individual needs is a perfectly appropriate prayer session to include in the group prayer retreat, and people are genuinely grateful if there is time at the end of the retreat for this kind of personalized prayer. However, attendees should know that individual needs will not be the focus of the bulk of the time spent in prayer.

Despite clearly communicating this, you may still encounter someone who comes to a corporate prayer retreat who is needy, hurting, and perhaps desperate. Given their state of mind and heart, when they realize they are going to be in the presence of a group of prayer warriors assembled to intercede, they may not be able to resist the temptation to try to shift the prayer focus to their own personal needs throughout the time together. Again, this is rare, but if you do find someone who seems very emotionally fragile, who relates every prayer topic mentioned to their own personal situation, who overshares their own drama or inserts their personal needs into the prayer sessions by asking for personal prayer or wanting the attention to be on their hurts and needs, you will need to address this. Usually, pulling them aside with another leader or mature attendee and praying over them while the others engage in the prayer topics for that particular session will assuage their need for care and comfort and enable them to fold back into the group agenda. Alternatively, you can remind people early in the agenda that there will be a time at the end of the retreat where individual needs will be addressed and lifted in prayer, with an encouragement to stay focused on intercession on the general topics that the group developed in the discerning session.

WHAT IF A SPIRIT OF GOSSIP IS CLEARLY PRESENT?

One of the challenges that groups may face when they begin to intercede for those not present is how to effectively share prayer needs without gossiping. The difficulty lies in knowing at what point sharing information devolves into gossip, since gossip is often information based in truth or even wholly true. Whereas slander, which is spreading untrue rumors or false information about others, is easier to avoid since it entails making stuff up or passing along unsubstantiated or confirmed information, (which most believers find completely unacceptable), gossip is repeating something that is true about a person. A good rule of thumb is this: if the person has shared publicly about the situation and asked for prayer in group settings, then it can be shared as a prayer need with the group; but if the situation was shared in confidence or is *not* widely known, then it should not be brought up in a public space. Assume that such knowledge should be held privately unless the individual who is the subject of the prayer need has given explicit permission for the need to be shared, or has personally shared the need publicly.

Another way to avoid gossip is to keep the prayer topics general in nature—marriages, relationships with children, jobs, financial stability, addictions, etc. are all worthy prayer topics to post on the whiteboard or poster paper under any of the categories of ministry, church, world, or potpourri/miscellaneous, without calling out individuals to whom this category applies. As with other pitfalls that a leader might have to face, a spirit of gossip is not a common occurrence. But it is more likely with certain groups or individuals that may be young in age or at varying levels of spiritual maturity. As we remember that the enemy is highly opposed to God's children gathering to intercede in prayer, we should not be surprised that Satan will use any tactic he can to misdirect our prayers or activate our carnal thinking and behaving. Mindful of the works of the enemy, you the leader can be watchful, aware of the ways that he might seek to intervene. This is where we heed the verse 1 Peter 1:8 (NKJV), which says, *"Be sober, be vigilant; because your adversary the devil walks about like a roaring lion, seeking whom he may devour."* As the leader, you are not afraid of the devil, but you are aware and prepared to deal with whatever ways he may try to derail your holy time of prayer.

> Another way to avoid gossip is to keep the prayer topics general in nature...

CHAPTER NINE

CONCLUSION

> "One of the greatest weaknesses in churches today, I believe, is the fact that Christians don't pray together... I dare to believe that as Christians learn more about prayer and actually pray together, they will discover for themselves new oceans of corporate prayer."
> —Carolyn Rhea, *Come Pray with Me: The Power of Praying Together*. (Grand Rapids: Zondervan, 1977), preface.

Well, you've come to the end of this Guidebook. I hope that it has been the right balance of motivation and explanation. My goal was to keep it short enough that even those who don't enjoy reading and rarely pick up a book would be willing to read it, while providing enough information that those wishing to lead a retreat would be equipped with the "why" as well as the "how." I hope I was able to reach you, even if you consider yourself a reluctant reader! I also realize that some people are voracious consumers of literature, capable of processing a lot of heady information very quickly. If that describes you, you may have wanted a deeper theological rationale, or more references and footnotes so that you could hear other voices or experts weighing in on the various topics covered here. For those types of readers, I did not intend this book to have a more academic or scholarly approach. Here we are, though, and you folks are still reading, so at least you didn't count it as too common to finish. And for that, I thank you. But really, if either reluctant or voracious readers simply *read* it, my ultimate goal will not have been met. What I want more than anything from writing this book is for individuals to take a leap of faith and plan a prayer retreat—that one you'd like to have that perhaps was the impetus for procuring this book. My effort will have been worth it if it spurs individuals such as yourself to the joyful work of planning and implementing a prayer retreat. So, please, don't just finish the book, add it to your list of books you've read this year, then put it on a shelf where you will never touch it again.

Instead, PLEASE begin a conversation with a friend or colleague or two. Tell them, *"I just finished this book about the whys and wherefores of leading a group prayer retreat. I think it would be something our ministry /group/ team would find really beneficial. What do you think? Can we talk more about it?"* Please have that conversation. And pray. Ask God what your next steps should be. Ask Him to reveal if a prayer retreat is something to which He wants you to call your friends and/or colleagues, much like I did (yes, even if you must ask in fear and trembling!). Ponder whether this is the Lord's leading and ask Him for direction. I shared with you some of my prayer journey over the last several decades, leading to a dissertation on corporate prayer after three years of reading, writing, studying, and thinking about this topic. I have been convinced more than ever of the importance of God's people praying together. Yet I also am convicted that, at least in my experience, most followers of Jesus spend very little time praying with other people, interceding for the needs of the church, their communities, for the world.

What might God do if His people were to commit anew to making space, planning to expend the time, energy, and resources to promote times of extended corporate prayer? What would happen in our lives, in our families, in our ministries and our churches if prayer retreats were normalized? What if we regularly, as a part of the church calendar, spent hours in prayer together, led by the Holy Spirit, informed by the Scriptures, in a strategic model that imbued purpose and design into the gatherings? Could we see breakthrough? Could our lives be transformed? Could we see the Kingdom come on earth as it is in heaven? I believe we could—maybe not after one retreat, or two, or three—but maybe so. I know that God delights in our giving to Him the loaves and fish we possess in order to see the miracles He would work to feed His people. He takes our offering, however meager, however imperfect, and multiplies it beyond our comprehension.

So step out. As you pray about planning a prayer retreat, don't despise the day of small beginnings. Decades ago, my husband and I went away with another couple to spend twenty-four hours in prayer. We jumped into the car on a Friday night as soon as everyone had finished their work day and had settled the children with sitters, and then headed to a beach house two-plus hours away. We had a glorious time of prayer in the car ride there. We parked the car in the driveway of the rental, heaved our suitcases out of the trunk, and realized we had left the rental house key back home. Ugh.

> "Do not despise the day of small beginnings, for the Lord rejoices to see the work begin."
> Zech. 4:10(NKJV)

However, the Lord gave us grace and peace to make the round-trip home and back again—praying every mile of the way. It was a quick overnight, but the Holy Spirit was powerfully present during that short time as we interceded for our church, for our children, and for each other. Perhaps your first prayer retreat will be similar (minus forgetting the house key, I hope), just you and a few friends, or your spouse and another couple. Or perhaps the Lord will give you favor with your leader because your ministry is in a time of crisis, or because your leader is a big proponent of prayer such that your first foray into leading a prayer retreat finds you with fifty attendees. Wow. That would be phenomenal, *and* come with some logistical challenges that would really require careful planning and forethought. But you can do it! You could take the template offered here and curate the most helpful pieces to shape your event. You are only limited by your willingness to be used in whatever capacity God has in mind. So dream big, dream small…but dream. And pray. And see what God would do.

APPENDIX A

EASY CHART: A SUMMARY OF ACTION STEPS	
*This and the other charts are available digitally at deborahjamiller.com	
BEFORE THE PRAYER RETREAT	
Hold a planning meeting.	Invite a small team to help you put on the event.
Set dates/secure facility.	In order to have the most options, start looking for venues and checking their calendars six to nine months before you want to have the event. This is not absolutely necessary but does give you time to search for the right venue.
Send early announcements/ongoing communication.	Before finalizing the dates (and venue) you may want to send an early calendar check to the people essential to have in attendance to

Planning a Prayer Retreat

	ascertain their availability. Once the date and place are set, even with a small group, know what you need to communicate and when you need to communicate it, and designate someone (it may be you) to be responsible to push those reminders and notifications out.
Hold registration.	Gather commitments to attend. At a minimum, get name, contact information, sleeping preference, and food allergies.
Send packing list and BASIC agenda.	When to show up and when it's over; what to bring (Bible, journal, a snack to share, etc.).
Communicate the week of the event.	Reminder email with address (again) of location; reminder to check packing list.

DURING THE PRAYER RETREAT	
Leader(s) arrive and set up.	You've most likely done a pre-visit so you know the layout, so you don't need to arrive more than 60 to 90 minutes in advance to unpack food, set up the general meeting area (your worship team should arrive thirty minutes to forty-five minutes before start time) and be sure the rooms are ready. You can put names on the door, or if you have notes for the attendees or name designations for the room, put those up. If you have not done a pre-visit, plan to come two hours early to establish your group gathering space, get the kitchen organized (or support those who are doing that), and be sure the place is ready for the attendees when they arrive. Be sure to set up the white board or easels, have a table with sticky notes if you plan to use them, and scope out areas for small group prayer.

Planning a Prayer Retreat

Attendees arrive—get them settled.	Greet attendees and provide general instructions for sleeping arrangements. Let the group explore before the official start time.
Food preparation.	Be sure meal coordinator is ready with dinner plans; set out beverages; plan your snack area.
Begin the retreat in your large group prayer area.	Welcome. Give **overview** of schedule (don't try to walk through every point of the agenda. People won't remember and most will be bored.) Tell them when dinner will be and when the first session starts. (If this is the first session, tell them you will be having worship and then giving more specific prayer details on the agenda)
Engage in worship.	Team should have set up for worship at least thirty minutes in advance OR facilitator should have digital worship ready to go (website, small speaker and designated phone and playlist, etc.).

Walk through the rhythm of the prayer sessions.	Don't over explain, but give basic structure.
Explain the discerning activity and send out to discern prayer topics.	Hand out sticky notes before you disperse everyone, if you plan to use them.
Come back together and have attendees share prayer topics. Post sticky notes on white board, grouping into categories. Target the first two prayer topics.	Give a short break after this time, if necessary.
Break into small prayer groups. Assign first prayer topic. Send out; bring back; give next topic, send out, bring back.	For each of the small group prayer sessions, you will typically do two prayer assignments in a row, then take a break or do something different in the schedule—a meal, worship, debriefing, etc.
Based on your window of time, do at least one more set of prayer topics before dinner.	If you have time for a full three hours of prayer before dinner, then do it. Most groups will only have time for one or two, depending on

Planning a Prayer Retreat

	how late in the day they are able to get started on day one.
Have dinner.	This can be done by people designated to provide meals who are not part of the prayer event, or you can have one group fixing the meal during the last prayer session before dinner. For longer retreats, you can give free time while groups rotate through meal prep and clean up since you will have more time for dedicated prayer than just an overnighter.
Engage in worship.	
Hold prayer session—two topics.	
Hold prayer session if it isn't too late and people are up for another round of topics OR do a debrief of the prayer times.	
Do a short debriefing if you haven't already.	

Release to free time or bed time.	
Have breakfast.	Handle this as you did dinner—either use designated meal prep and clean-up crew external to the prayer group, or rotate through attendees.
Gather as a large group after breakfast or simply remind people at breakfast that you are starting with a personal devotional time. Encourage attendees to spend time alone with God.	
Gather the large group together. Remind them the format will be worship and then prayer sessions.	As you look at your time of departure and the number of prayer topics left, make some executive decisions about how many prayer sessions you have left, and how many topics will need to be covered. During the first prayer session, you can group similar topics or decide to assign different topics to different groups. I always try

Planning a Prayer Retreat

	to cover all the topics that were shared as a way to honor the discerning process with which the group began.
Engage in worship.	
Assign prayer topics and work through the remaining topics, giving breaks between each set of two prayer topics.	Assigning two topics at a time is intended to fill an hour of prayer, give or take fifteen minutes. Giving breaks between each hour of prayer for bathroom use, to get snacks or drinks, or just to stretch is a good idea.
Take a morning break after the first prayer session.	HAVE ATTENDEES PACK THEIR BAGS SO THEY ARE READY TO GO AT RETREAT'S END
Hold final prayer session (the number of prayer sessions will vary this day, day two or later, depending on the length of your prayer retreat).	You may have decided to designate this session to focus on individual prayer needs. Be sure to set it up so that you can stay within the timeframe designated (see the narrative for suggestions for how to do this.)
Have closing debrief and benediction.	Try really hard to make time for at least a short debriefing to capture final takeaways and speak a blessing over your attendees.

Clean up, load cars, head-out.	You will most likely be the last person to leave, as you will want to make sure everything is picked up throughout the house (if a house was used) or in the general meeting area and small group prayer locations, as well as the kitchen and dining area. Communicate with the host, if one is present. Save the sticky notes from the white board or take photos of the white board. Be sure musicians have retrieved all power cords and equipment and instruments. Check the refrigerator. Remove the garbage, if necessary. Sweep the bathrooms and bedrooms for any left items.

AFTER THE PRAYER RETREAT	
Write a summary of anything you changed "on the fly" so you will remember what you did differently than you had planned.	Keep all notes related to anything about the Prayer Retreat in a digital file for easy access to share or for "next time."
Send out an evaluation/ feedback form to attendees to gather reflections.	Send within a week of the event. Consider using a reputable survey site or some digital version for easy data analysis and storage of responses in your Prayer Retreat file. NOTE: do not be gut punched by "Negative Nellies" or outlier critical comments. Sift through the feedback with the Holy Spirit at your right hand!
Report the fruit of the experience to your church leader(s).	This reinforces the value of the experience, especially if the church supported the event with funds; it also can encourage the pastor or other staff to consider taking a prayer retreat with their respective groups.

APPENDIX B

SAMPLE RETREAT SCHEDULE

VANCOUVER CHURCH WOMEN'S LEADERSHIP PRAYER RETREAT TIMELINE

OCTOBER 18-19, 2024

TIME	ACTIVITY	NOTES
FRIDAY		
3:30	Abby and Deborah Arrive to Prep Missy sets up for worship by 5:00	Food arrives and prepares dinner; sets up snacks and beverages
5:00	Women arrive and settle in to their rooms; prepare for dinner	Assign rooms as people arrive; just let people know which rooms are available and they can select roommates. Help, if needed.
5:30-6:05	Dinner	Lynn and her team will prepare, serve, and clean up
6:10-6:40	Worship	Missy will lead

Planning a Prayer Retreat

6:40-6:55	Explain the agenda and the opening exercise	
7:00-7:30	Personal prayer time of seeking God for three prayer foci with scriptures	Women should do this on their own, not in groups; give note cards/sticky notes
7:30-8:00	Come back together and generate a prayer list to govern the retreat prayer times	Need white paper and pens or whiteboard/pens to organize prayer topics for the retreat
8:05-8:30	Assign to groups and send out with **first prayer focus**; if necessary, provide guidelines for prayer time (limit "talking" about the prayer focus; pray together—not just each one takes a turn to pray the list)	Each group chooses location and will "popcorn" pray for this topic
8:35-8:40	Come back together to get the next item and then redeploy	

8:40-9:05	**Second prayer focus**	
9:10-9:15	Re-gather to get next prayer focus	
9:15-9:45	**Third prayer focus**	
9:45—10:25	Gather for debrief and worship time	
10:30	Fellowship and bedtime as desired	
SATURDAY		
7:30-8:00	Breakfast	Lynn and crew
8:00-8:30	Personal Prayer Time	Process with the Lord your thoughts, feelings, desires, and needs.
8:30-8:55	Worship	Missy and Deborah
8:55-9:00	Reassign prayer teams and send out with fourth prayer focus	
9:00-9:30	**Fourth prayer with groups**	
9:30-9:35	Regroup and get next topic	
9:40-10:05	**Fifth prayer with groups**	

Planning a Prayer Retreat

10:10-10:25	Break and next topic	
10:25-10:50	**Sixth prayer with groups**	
10:55-11:55	Group prayer and debrief	This will be a time of praying for personal needs, prophetic words, or whatever

BIBLIOGRAPHY

Barry, Dan. "After the Attacks: The Vigils; Surrounded by Grief, People Around the World Pause and Turn to Prayer," September 15, 2001, *The New York Times*. Accessed at https://www.nytimes.com/2001/09/15/us/after-attacks-vigils-surrounded-grief-people-around-the-world-pause-turn-prayer.html.

Bounds, Edward M. *Prayer and Praying Men*. Grand Rapids: Baker Book House, 1977.

Brueggemann, Dale. "Corporate Prayer in the Old Testament," Sermons by Logos. Accessed July 24, 2024, at https://sermons.logos.com/sermons/345365-corporate-prayer-in-the-old-testament.

Curran, Sue. *The Praying Church, Principles & Power of Corporate Praying*. Lake Mary, FL: Creation House Press. 2001.

Cymbala, Jim. *Fresh Wind, Fresh Fire*. Grand Rapids: Zondervan, 2018.

Forsyth, P.T. *The Soul of Prayer*, Waterford: CrossReach Publications, 2020. Originally published as *The Soul of Prayer*, London: C.H. Kelly, 1916.

Gardiner, David E. "The Miracle of Dunkirk," Christians Together, Accessed January 30, 2024 https://www.christianstogether.net/Articles/200052/Christians_Together_in/Christian_Life/The_Miracle_of.aspx.

Gundersen, Dennis. *A Praying Church: The Neglected Blessing of Corporate Prayer.* Sand Springs: Grace and Truth Books, 2019.

Hamilton, Jim. "A Biblical Theology of Corporate Prayer." Accessed 11.11.2022 at https://www.9marks.org/article/biblical-theology-corporate-prayer.

Lawler, Howard. *The Corporate Prayer Challenge.* Wake Forest, NC: Salpize Publications, 2020.

Miller, Paul E. *A Praying Church, Becoming a People of Hope in a Discouraging World.* Wheaton: Crossway, 2023.

Rhea, Carolyn. *Come Pray with Me: The Power of Praying Together.* Grand Rapids: Zondervan, 1977.

Smed, John. *Prayer Revolution: Rebuilding Church and City Through Prayer.* Chicago: Moody Publishers, 2020.

Spurgeon, Charles. *Only a Prayer Meeting: Studies on Prayer Meetings and Prayer Meeting Addresses.* Fearn, Scotland: Christian Heritage, 2010.

Winward, Stephen F. *Teach Yourself to Pray.* London: Hodder, 1961.

About Kharis Publishing:

Kharis Publishing, an imprint of Kharis Media LLC, is a leading Christian and inspirational book publisher based in Aurora, Chicago metropolitan area, Illinois. Kharis' dual mission is to give voice to under-represented writers (including women and first-time authors) and equip orphans in developing countries with literacy tools. That is why, for each book sold, the publisher channels some of the proceeds into providing books and computers for orphanages in developing countries so that these kids may learn to read, dream, and grow. For a limited time, Kharis Publishing is accepting unsolicited queries for nonfiction (Christian, self-help, memoirs, business, health and wellness) from qualified leaders, professionals, pastors, and ministers. Learn more at: https://kharispublishing.com/

www.ingramcontent.com/pod-product-compliance
Lightning Source LLC
Chambersburg PA
CBHW070158100426